MINDGAMES

RISING ABOVE OTHER PEOPLE'S CRAZINESS

MINDGAMES
RISING ABOVE OTHER PEOPLE'S CRAZINESS

BILL GIOVANNETTI

A LifeStyle Commentary on ESTHER

ENDURANT PRESS

MINDGAMES: RISING ABOVE OTHER PEOPLE'S CRAZINESS
A LIFESTYLE COMMENTARY ON ESTHER.

Endurant Press

ISBN Print edition: 978-1-946654-00-7

ATTENTION CORPORATIONS, UNIVERSITIES, COLLEGES, CHURCHES and MINISTRY GROUPS: Quantity discounts are available on bulk purchases of this book for educational, gift purposes, group studies, or premiums. Special books or book excerpts can also be created to fit specific needs. Please visit www.maxgrace.com for information.

CONTENTS

Dedication

For Josie

Being your father has brought me more joy than you'll ever know.
I am so proud to be your dad. Thank you for creating beauty,
laughter, and love in our family and in our world. I pray you
always let your inner royalty shine.
You are destined for a wonderful life.
Go be Josie.

I love you forever and ever...

LifeStyle Commentary Introduction

My friend's eyes grew wide, he shook his head, and laughed at the gift I'd just given him.

He said, "Bill, that's the biggest book I've ever seen."

His name was Josh, and I had just given him a Bible. Josh had just trusted Christ as his Savior, and wanted to know what was next. So I gave him a Bible.

Josh shook his head again and looked up at me. "Bill, I've never even read one book, and this is the biggest book I've ever seen."

As an avid reader, I couldn't imagine making it to my twenties without ever having read a book.

But his point was an eye-opener for me, a young pastor.

The Bible really is an imposing book. It's the biggest book most people have ever seen. Being given a Bible can feel like being given a box of jumbled up parts for a rocket ship, with orders to put the thing together and fly to Mars, without instructions.

This *LifeStyle Commentary* is written for people like Josh, and for you, if you see the Bible as an intimidating jumble of mysterious parts. Where to begin? What to do? How to use it?

A *commentary* takes a book or section of Scripture, and goes through it patiently, paragraph by paragraph, and verse by verse. I'll make comments as we go through the book, hence the name.

So that's what we'll do. We will be true to God's Word, and we will be real and authentic about how it relates to our lives. This *LifeStyle Commentary* assumes that you don't have a Bible degree, and might be a beginner in your life with God.

This is not a technical commentary. We will not delve into history or grammar or setting or Hebrew or Greek, except when it's needed to understand the point. I'll make it painless, I promise.

If we can dig in together to a section of God's perfect Word, and explore how by it God might transform our hearts and lives, then this commentary will have achieved its purpose.

So let's open just one bite-sized portion of God's Word and focus on real life, and on how the eternal truths of Scripture can help you live your life to the fullest.

Dr. Bill Giovannetti
Redding, CA

CHAPTER 1

Meet Other People's Craziness

HE DOESN'T WANT ME?

A hot tear escaped his swollen eyelid and rolled down his cheek. Every breath made his chest burn. He clutched his threadbare blanket and covered his head with his pillow. Only the pale moon witnessed the curled-up boy as the sound of another fight penetrated his bedroom door.

He told himself it would be okay, but his seven-year old brain knew better. He pushed hard, but his pillow couldn't drown out the noise.

Something crashed. His mother cried. His dad shouted. She yelled. They had long since given up muffling their voices for the boy's sake.

"Where were you? It's after midnight!"

"If I thought you cared about me, I wouldn't stay out so late!"

The boy squeezed his eyes shut and tried not to listen. He never understood the fights.

Then he heard the words that made his eyes open wide. They shot through his mental fog with piercing clarity. "I want a divorce," said his dad. "You can have the house. You can have the car. You can have the boy. I don't want anything."

The boy's mind entered another dimension. The clock on his nightstand ticked in half-time, like it was slogging through sludge. His clenched teeth hurt. He could hear a fly buzzing against the window.

My dad doesn't want me.

Instantly, consciously, purposely, the boy raised his shields. *I will not let them hurt me.* In his emotions he divorced them long before they could divorce each other.

Fast forward. Decades later, happily married with six children and a bubbly granddaughter, his struggles with intimacy seem like somebody else's nightmare. He bears the scars of other people's brokenness, but those scars no longer define him. He's gotten past them. This book describes how you can too.

𐤟 𐤟 𐤟 𐤟 𐤟 𐤟

A little girl enjoys a tea party with her dolls. Her mom calls for the third time, "Let's go, and I mean right now! Put your shoes on or we'll be late for church."

The girl pauses for a final sip of tea.

Big mistake.

Her mother bursts into the room. "I said put your shoes on. We're leaving now!" The mother grabs a curly-haired doll, rips the head off, and hurls it across the room.

The girl freezes.

"I said put your shoes on!"

She races to find them. Her mind shuts down. Her eyes can't focus; her mom's voice sounds muffled. *Where are my shoes?* She looks in the closet where they belong. Her mother screams words at her, but she hears only noise. She scours the hallway with her eyes. She searches under her bed. She can't find them. Her body shudders.

"I said put your shoes on!"

"But I can't find them!"

Then comes the accusation she'd heard a thousand times before. "Why do you have to be so stupid!"

Pieces of her heart drop into an abyss. Soon she will seal it shut.

Sitting silently at church she examines her distorted reflection in her shiny shoes while her smiling mother sings the hymn. No one suspects the storm savaging her spirit.

I'll show you how smart I am.

Her life tells the tale of an overachiever. She studies hard. Gets the best grades. Flies through college and medical school. Rises to the top.

And hates every minute of it.

She can't remember why she is so driven. Perfectionism and workaholism pull apart her marriage. She's trying to impress somebody, but can't remember who. She's shocked to realize that her husband makes her feel stupid, too.

What force in her heart made her choose him?

Others, in their moments of weakness, defined her.

Fast forward. A painful divorce and a faltering reconciliation with her mother inspire a revelation: she doesn't have to accept her mother's caustic definitions. She's never had to. She's always had the power to embrace beautiful new labels from God.

Today, as a successful doctor, she enjoys helping others tap into that same power. She's made peace with her ex. Her children thrive in their marriages and career. She's made peace with her past and with God. No longer driven to impress, an image of wholeness and sanity has replaced the distortions of her childhood.

As we trace the hesitant steps of a journey like hers, I'm confident that you'll discover your own steps to wholeness.

One more case study.

𖤐 𖤐 � 𖤐 𖤐 𖤐

A little boy sits frozen in the warm, foamy bath water. This is supposed to be fun. Lots of toys and splashes.

Instead he feels exposed and vulnerable. He doesn't understand these feelings and doesn't know why he has them. All he knows is that the family member entrusted with his bath this night is doing some things he shouldn't. It's wrong, but the boy doesn't know why.

Nor does he know that this would be the first time of many. Or that he would grow to like it even as he grows to hate himself.

The boy chokes down a gut-wrenching panic. He wants to shout, but no words come. His chest feels paralyzed.

Where's my dad? he wonders. *How come my dad's not here? I need my dad!* The boy has never felt more abandoned.

He doesn't understand what happened to him. His mind forgets, but his soul remembers.

He feels dirty and lashes back with anger. He searches for a fatherly bond, but sexualizes that search. His confusion frightens him.

Someone else's evil has altered his personality.

Fast forward. As a husband, father, and acclaimed musician, he confesses that it was his wife who empowered him to fight against that evil. How? She introduced him to God, the only Father who never abandoned him.

In this book we reveal how an encounter with God can overcome any amount of dysfunction and enable even the most confused spirit to reclaim its truest identity. It's not easy—the fight is hard. But it's winnable, and this book is dedicated to showing you how.

Having struggles: normal.

Not being dominated by them: priceless.

𐤔 𐤚 𝍏 ⟪ 𐤔 ⟩⟪

Sometimes, other people's craziness is more than we can bear. You've been there, right?

When I watched *Good Will Hunting,* I got choked up when the therapist, Sean (Robin Williams), hugged the troubled youth, Will (Matt Damon), assuring him "It's not your fault. It's not your fault. It's not your fault."

Is it so bad for me to want some of that?

A lot of people threw their ingredients into the stew of who I am. Not all of it good. Some of it downright evil. I don't want to nurture a victim-mentality, but I do want to get in touch with reality. The reality is that Other People's Craziness has affected me profoundly. And I am treated to more doses of it every single day.

When my life gets crazy, much of the time it is my own dumb fault. I admit it. My bad.

But it's certainly not *all* my fault. And the mess in your life is not all your fault either. A lot of people have done a lot of bad things to you. They have pushed you into a tragic story.

So why is it always you on the hot seat? For once, can't we put the heat on all the crazy people who've been messing with you and yours?

Let's go after the crazy-making world of mindgames and the people who play them.

Other People's Craziness—next to your own craziness—is the biggest splat on the windshield of your life. Let's stipulate that we create enough of our own craziness to occupy a small army of therapists. There are plenty of books, seminars and therapists to sermonize about your particular "issues." But let's give you a break. Let's sermonize about the other guy for once, okay?

Consider yourself "off the hook" for however long it takes to read this book. I'm not after confession, repentance, guilt, or shame from you. I'm not after you at all.

I'm after the people in your life who do bad stuff to you, and the forces in your heart that let them get away with it. Yes, these people pushed you in a certain direction, but you have the power to change trajectory.

I want to show you how to have a great life in spite of Other People's Craziness. I am totally confident in these principles. Not because I'm a sage or anything like that. I am confident because of their source. The principles in this book come from the Bible, specifically the book of Esther.

Esther, a beautiful, smart woman, is one of the toughest people you'll ever meet. Her story bristles with palace intrigue, a murderous plot, and bad guys getting what's coming to them in violent acts of revenge. Esther is not the only character in the story. There's an ancient Al Capone named King Xerxes, a would-be Hitler named Haman, and a King Arthur named Mordecai.

Other People's Craziness (OPC) messes with men and women equally—it's an epidemic. Thankfully, God has given us his wisdom on how to smash OPC into a gooey little mess. Every follower of Christ can access that wisdom in God's Word, the Bible.

We're almost ready to enter the palace garden with Esther. First, let's put some names to the craziness she has to face.

CHAPTER 2

What is Other People's Craziness

OTHER PEOPLE'S CRAZINESS encompasses all the bad stuff other people do to you without a righteous cause. OPC springs forth from their immaturity, insecurity, selfishness, arrogance, corruption, evil, or dysfunction. It includes all the hurts, threats, and aggravations you deal with every day. If it causes you grief, and somebody else is doing it, and you don't have it righteously coming to you, then it's OPC.

Most of us will be able to sniff out four cesspools of OPC in our lives: Family, Work, Social Networks, and The System.

Family OPC

Your dad gambles the family into bankruptcy. No matter how much your mom works, she can't bring in enough. When they visit, he acts like nothing's wrong. When your neighbor's pretty wife strolls by, you watch your dad eye her up and down. Like always, your mom just goes to her happy place.

Your mom gushes over your sister's new hairstyle, not saying a word about yours. Then she zings you with one of her classic compliments: "The pork roast is really tasty, even though it's a little dry." You flash back to mixed praise for your kindergarten art.

Parental OPC towers over other sources in its impact. It defaces your self-image and launches you on a lifelong quest for unconditional love and unmixed praise.

That quest easily spills over from family OPC into marital OPC.

How many gallons of emotional fuel do some couples burn each day on their spouse's craziness in the bathroom only? Seat up, seat down. Toilet paper unrolls from the top or the bottom. Do you think your dirty laundry is going to crawl by itself into the hamper? Do you have to flood the whole bathroom when you shower? Leave some hot water for me. Don't squeeze the tube in the middle. There's a little lever here, and if you push it, it *flushes*—you should try it once in a while.

And that's just one room.

The Psalmist boasts, "I will lead a life of integrity in my own home" (Psalm 101:2). But then he didn't marry a certifiable nut like you did.

Nowhere does marital OPC manifest itself more than in your bedroom. Or in the bedroom of the person with whom your good-for-nothing spouse had an affair. Enough said.

Sexual OPC manifests itself in pornography, affairs, promiscuity, sexual-deviance, flirtatiousness, inhibited sexual desire, fetishes, non-medically caused impotence, and a lot of other practices. Whatever the manifestation, if you married it, you're the one living with it. This can be devastating.

I'm not knocking marriage. It's a great blessing. God intends it for your pleasure. Your fun. Your healing. Married sex is a blast. Kids need married parents whenever possible. Society needs married families. Marriage is a gift from God. I love being married. And I love my wife and kids.

But marriage is also the riskiest step you'll ever take because of the way it magnifies OPC. So choose carefully. Be willing to live with the OPC you choose, because I guarantee your spouse has been infected, at least a little. To some degree, we all have.

Even so, your partner's craziness—whether mild and adorable or severe and scary—is not your fault.

Marital OPC invariably gets transmitted to your kids (not from you, but from your crazy ex- or your dysfunctional spouse—we're not talking about you, remember?). Despite your best intentions, infestations of OPC scurry from limb to limb of your family tree.

Don't worry, though. Your kids will return your OPC investment with compound interest—as surly teenagers and young adults, telling the world of your vast array of failures through social media. It all comes around.

In its mild forms, family OPC can be endearing, quirky, and cute. If Grandpa didn't leave his toenails on the end table, if Aunt Alice didn't pull out her teeth for the kids, and if cousin Karl no longer licked the ketchup drip off the bottle, what fun would holiday dinners be? The crazy stuff—when it's mild— makes your family worth a visit.

But in extreme forms, family OPC wreaks havoc on tender psyches and leaves a legacy of woundedness that can last a lifetime—unless you discover the secrets of rising above Other People's Craziness.

Workplace/School OPC

When your boss drags her boatload of OPC into the office and screeches at you for a late report, all you can do is back into the corner of your cage and lick your wounds like a stressed-out Schnoodle. You need your job, so you grin and bear it, day after day. This makes you edgy when you hit the gym or finally get home to your spouse and kids. But it's not your fault. Honestly, you're a decent person and nobody knows the trouble you've seen.

Job satisfaction in America has plummeted over the last three decades. A majority of employees are dissatisfied with their careers.

Could OPC account for this? Could obsessive bosses, pressured by stressed-out upper management, make workplaces a living hell for humble underlings who just want to make a decent living and be able to afford a fancy dinner once in a while?

Let's not even get started with technology. Devices. Operating systems. Painful upgrades, spreadsheets, texting, syncing, networking, and the I.T. department.

And O.S.H.A. and regulators and environmental laws.

And what about customers? Some of them are great. Thank God for them. But others crawled out from under a rock just to torment you.

What low life-form would return tires to a store he didn't buy them from? When a customer in Fairbanks, Alaska returned four car tires to Nordstrom's, the clerk reached into the till and refunded the money. Nordstrom's has never sold tires. The customer gleefully accepted the refund, most likely guaranteeing his reservation in the hottest part of hell.[1]

Bad customers are what happen when implacability collides with miserliness and then splits to form a bad-tipper and an early-bird diner. They're not looking for dinner. Or a supplier. Or merchandise.

They're looking for a mommy. And you have to suckle them. It's your job. So sorry.

Same with the ant colony commonly known as school. All you want is to get an education and have a good time (not necessarily in that order). Yet you spend your days distracted by that creepy classmate from Sociology who leers at you when he thinks you're not looking and always ends up at the same table as you in the cafe-gym-natorium. You've told your R.A., but there's nothing she can do.

What about the girl who flirted with you and dumped you? Or the guy who flirted with you and turned out to be gay? Let's not even talk about those infamous "mean girls."

Schools breed OPC like Petri dishes breed staphylococci.

Enough crazy energy comes at you from your workplace or school to fuel a rocket ship to Mars.

Unfortunately the OPC doesn't stop there.

Social Network OPC

Facebook, Instagram, Twitter, Snapchat, dating sites—even stretching back to misty memories of MySpace—social media strains every day, laboring to birth its prolific brood of craziness.

But it's not just online.

A few years back, while working in a previous church, I was served a healthy heaping of Social Network OPC in the form of a Homeowners Association. I had just arrived at my office, a forty-minute commute from home, when my wife phoned, sobbing. She was 35 weeks pregnant with our first child, so my emotions leaped to DEFCON one. Between sobs, my articulate, bright attorney and wife blurted out something like, "The men from the... ah... ah... homeowners' association came and said... sniff... that our new fence... snort!... doesn't conform to the bylaws... blachawahwah... and we have to tear it... down... waaaaahhhh. I want to... ahhh... moooooove... ahahahah..."

Welcome to life in a suburban subdivision. We had just spent $1,800.00 on a new fence around the back yard of our new house. My next-door neighbor lodged a complaint that it didn't conform to the precious bylaws. Never mind that I had cleared the fence design with the President of the homeowners' association three times via phone. It didn't matter. Three mealy-mouthed male officers of the homeowners' association knocked at my door during business hours, armed with tape measures, knowing that I'd be gone and my wife would be home alone.

Never mind that the fence was beautiful—split-rail cedar with a black wire mesh. Never mind that it exceeded the neighborhood standard of chain link. Or that, due to a sloping yard, only four feet of it was visible from the sidewalk. Or that the sacred bylaws required said fence if we had dogs (how I wish my wife had just released the hounds).

Never mind all that. Some nosy neighbor didn't like it, so the Knights of Fence Rectitude Templar convened in a smoke-filled room in the dark of night to plot their foray to my front door so they could pronounce their findings to my vulnerable wife not seven days into our new home.

"Your fence posts are one inch too high. Tear them down."

I am not making this up.

After the smoke cleared—fence intact—I found out to my extreme gratification that my neighbor's wife really laid into him for making a pregnant woman cry. He later extended an apology, which I accepted with punishingly detached cordiality.

My wife is still working on forgiveness. Our daughter is in high school.

Wherever two or three people are gathered, Social Network OPC will be in their midst.

Think of social networks as all the places you go or browse when you're not working, attending classes, sleeping, or at home. Wherever people congregate, OPC flourishes: in every store, subdivision, school, gym, club, tavern, coffee house, synagogue, forum, website comment section, and church. It hangs out in singles groups and senior citizen centers. High school youth-groups and church-based small groups.

Even your friends have it. Shall we recount the times our friends have let us down? Sure, why not! There was the time my ex-best friend flirted with and planted a reputedly juicy kiss on my ex-girlfriend. And the time one of my wife's ex-best friends gossiped a spiteful slander about my wife to a friend of a friend of a friend and it got back to us from 2,309 miles away.

OPC is OPC, even from your friends. Your social networks teem with it.

But it gets even worse. Because you don't just have to deal with other people's craziness, sometimes, the system sends OPC your way too.

Systemic OPC

A congressional aid told me of a paper mill in a nearby town that wanted to harvest the unscorched timber in the aftermath of a forest fire. Delay would make the timber unusable.

Enter the Federal Forestry Department.

I love my country. I sing along with the national anthem at sporting events. I am an unashamed, flag-waving American.

But federal departments are another story.

The Forestry Department, a.k.a. the Federal Department for the Protection of Dead Things, worried that if the mill harvested dead trees they might kill nearby dead vegetation. Plus, it wouldn't be good for the dead trees.

Logging permit denied.

Now, who's to blame for such insanity? A department. The Congress. The local Forestry Department division. The problem is that everybody's just doing their jobs. The mill operator was spitting mad, but had nobody to be mad at.

This California paper mill continues to import trees from New Zealand to produce paper.

Crazy.

Call it the System or The Man or Fate. When something's driving you crazy, and you can't put a name to it, turn over a few dead logs and you'll find Systemic OPC.

I'll put disease and random crime into this category too. Racism. Sexism. All the other −isms and phobias. Ditto with hurricanes, earthquakes, and tornadoes. They may be called "acts of God," but you're unlikely to get much satisfaction if you yell at him.

Who's to blame? The System. The Man. Nobody. Everybody.

I am so sorry.

It's not your fault. Others may blame you. They may look down their superior noses and whisper of your foibles and failures. But not me. I don't blame you. I don't shame you. I'm on your side. Crazies on your left. Crazies on your right. I get it. I'm proud you've made it this far without becoming a newspaper headline.

𒐁𒌋𒈠𒐊𒐁𒁹

Other People's Craziness is a genuine phenomenon and I'm here to make it certifiable.

And, really, no heaps of guilt or shame. In the spirit of full disclosure, toward the later chapters of the book, we'll start pointing out what you can do. No, OPC is not your fault, but dealing with it becomes your responsibility. Bummer, I know. I'll be gentle.

And take hope! You are stronger, tougher, more determined, and more tenacious than you realize. You can tap into power you never knew you had. Esther's story shows the way.

So click off the glaring lamp. Arise from the hot seat. Step away from the third degree. You're free to go. It's not your fault. The butler did it. Your fence conforms.

Now, let's dig into an enduring story and start spreading blame for the misery in your life where it really belongs: on lots and lots of other people.

𒐁𒌋𒈠𒐊𒁹

Reflections

I'll follow each chapter with a couple of "Reflections." These are practical applications designed to spark group discussion or personal reflection.

Reflections 1: Understand the source of OPC—we live in a fallen world.

Other People's Craziness doesn't have rights to our world; it's an alien invader. God created a perfect world, and set the human race in a perfect environment. We blew it, corporately speaking. Our original parents fell into sin, and dragged everyone and everything down with them. Don't be too hard on Adam and Eve, though. Every day you prove that, if you were in their sandals, you would have made the same apocalyptic choice.

We can't blame God for it. He is not the author either of sin or its evil twin, OPC. We asked for it.

Sin introduced a moral twist into the fabric of all creation, including us. Old-time Christians called it a "corruption of nature." Today we call it "original sin" or "the old sin nature." Whatever you call it, it's the source of OPC and we brought it upon ourselves.

This fallen world is a morally broken pain machine.

And you're stuck inside it.

This means that the OPC events in your life are not unrelated bits of bad luck. They are, instead, the gnarled outgrowths of a single malignant root: sin. The good news is that God has a single solution, wrapped up in his Son, Jesus. More about him later.

Because sin, evil and OPC are invaders—and not core attributes of human nature—God can exterminate them without altering our essential humanness. He can restore our original innocence. He can reverse the effects of OPC. That's his plan, but it's going to take a while. So hang in there; a better day is coming.

FOR REFLECTION AND DISCUSSION: Does the Bible let us blame God for evil? What does James 1:13-16 say about that? Discuss or journal a time when you blamed God for some OPC that afflicted you.

Reflections 2: Don't be surprised by anybody's capacity to be crazy.

OPC is pandemic. Don't be shocked when it slithers from under its rock and strikes.

Even at our best, we can't restore Paradise. The world's brokenness hovers like a dark cloud over every silver lining. No matter how noble your neighbor, pastor, or spouse may be, they are still tainted by sin, and therefore capable of big-league craziness.

Unless you reconcile yourself to the fallen condition of the world, you'll join the Order of the Perpetually Peeved. Never satisfied, you'll zero in on the flaws of others like a heat-seeking missile.

The only way to stay afloat on this OPC-ocean called life is by accepting the inevitable. St. Peter taught: "Dear friends, don't be surprised at the fiery trials you are going through, as if something strange were happening to you" (1 Peter 4:12). Don't be surprised; your sanity depends on it.

FOR REFLECTION AND DISCUSSION: What does 1 Peter 4:8, 9 tell you about the universality of OPC? Discuss or journal 2 or 3 ways in which OPC has dramatically affected your life. Journal some life stories that illustrate each variety of OPC: family, workplace/school, social network, and the system.

CHAPTER 3

OPC and Your World

THE WOMAN SIGHED WITH SATISFACTION. Her gilded mirror reflected a flawless complexion, high cheekbones, and almond-shaped eyes. She ran her finger over scarlet lips— permitting a slight smile that hinted at sensuality and pleasure. Brushing back ebony hair, she revealed an arched neck on which she dabbed her husband's favorite scent. Satiny skin glowed from the flickering candlelight. Long lashes framed midnight eyes. The fire in those eyes revealed an inner strength.

On closer inspection, she saw the hint of a frown-line between her eyebrows. And deep in her eyes—had anyone else cared to look—she saw sadness and discontent. She set down the mirror.

Hers was a marriage of convenience. She knew that. She wasn't the only woman in his life. Her husband, rich and powerful, made no secret of the other women in his life.

But deep inside, she hoped that one day he would see her as more than just another toy in his collection.

At least I have my integrity, she told herself. She was right. She had honesty and toughness to match her beauty. Her husband respected that in her. She knew it.

But what she didn't know was that, at that very moment, at the far end of their estate, he was hatching a plan that would change her life. She must either sacrifice her dignity on the altar of his arrogance, or forever lose her wealth, her prestige, and the only life she has known.

Which will she choose?

⬚⚡〣⟪⬚⤛

Which would you choose? Sometimes, OPC is serious business.

No generation has ever been exempt from the curse of OPC. But that doesn't mean we should give up hope. We have access to the wisdom immortalized in the Book of Esther.

That trophy wife with the playboy husband and the looming crisis was named Vashti—Queen of the Persian Empire and an international beauty.

Her husband was King Xerxes, one of the most powerful and flamboyant rulers ever to walk the earth. Even though Vashti lived over 2,400 years ago, she struggled with the same kind of craziness that you and I struggle with today.

But I'm getting ahead of the story.

An Impressive World

The story begins with a party.

This happened in the days of King Xerxes, who reigned over 127 provinces stretching from India to Ethiopia. At that time he ruled his empire from his throne at the fortress of Susa.

31

In the third year of his reign, he gave a banquet for all his princes and officials. He invited all the military officers of Media and Persia, as well as the noblemen and provincial officials. The celebration lasted six months—a tremendous display of the opulent wealth and glory of his empire. (Esther 1:1-4)

"Party" doesn't do it justice. Bacchanalia is more like it. Six months of revelry, carousing, and enough food to make your FitBit explode. Hold that thought.

The Book of Esther is actual history. Ample evidence supports this view, but we'll leave that for other books. I also believe that nobody will ever solve the mystery of who wrote it. I'll refer to that mysterious man or woman either as the Author or the Storyteller. Since we can't be sure who it was, I'll call the Author a "she." Please, just go with it.

Plus, in case you wonder why some Bibles call him Ahasueras, most scholars accept this as simply another title for King Xerxes.

Enough prefacing—let's get back to the wow-factor bacchanalia.

A big party. So what? By describing Esther's world, the Author intends to describe your world. The capital of ancient Persia serves as a mini-world. Every-world. Think of it as your neighborhood, family, workplace, subdivision, dorm, apartment complex, school, or prison cell.

As the Author brings you deeper into the story, she invites you to consider her first big question: What is the nature of your world?

For Xerxes and his subjects, it's a very, very, very nice world.

But not all is paradise. We're only four verses into the story, and we can already detect a hint of Other People's Craziness.

Why does the king throw his party? Verse 4 notes that the king does so as a "a tremendous display of the opulent wealth and glory of his empire." The king is not motivated to do good to his subjects; he's motivated to boost his own image. His party serves his neediness.

As readers, we know that, because the Storyteller says so. But I wonder if his guests know that. What if they think the king wants to be good to them, when really he just wants to royally inflate his own ego?

The king's insecurities are showing and, when the guy who runs the show is insecure, it's only a matter of time before everybody's ducking for cover.

The glam-fest continues.

> When it was all over, the king gave a special banquet for all the palace servants and officials—from the greatest to the least. It lasted for seven days and was held at Susa in the courtyard of the palace garden. The courtyard was decorated with beautifully woven white and blue linen hangings, fastened by purple ribbons to silver rings embedded in marble pillars. Gold and silver couches stood on a mosaic pavement of porphyry, marble, mother-of-pearl, and other costly stones. Drinks were served in gold goblets of many designs, and there was an abundance of royal wine, just as the king had commanded. The only restriction on the drinking was that no one should be compelled to take more than he wanted. But those who wished could have as much as they pleased, for the king had instructed his staff to let everyone decide this matter for himself. (Esther 1:5-8)

[The following is not a political statement.] When Melania Knauss married Donald Trump, she wore a Christian Dior gown valued at over $200,000.00. It took twenty-eight seamstresses over 1,000 hours to make it. Ninety-eight yards of white satin embroidered with 1,500 pearls and crystal rhinestones. She dragged in her wake a thirteen-foot long train and a nineteen-foot long veil. The gown weighed over fifty pounds. She was encouraged to eat a lot so the heavy gown wouldn't make her pass out.

Melania wore custom made shoes with diamond encrusted ankle straps. Her 12-carat engagement ring was worth over $3 million.

The happy couple held their reception in a $42 million ballroom, featuring 24-karat-gold moldings and 11,000 square feet of marble flooring. Dinner featured Cristal champagne—about $400 per bottle—hors d'oeuvres, beef tenderloin and individual Grand Marnier chocolate truffle cakes.

The wedding cake itself stood five feet high, covered with 3,000 roses hand-crafted from white icing.

The centerpieces used over 10,000 flowers and cost over $1,000 each.

The guest list included Tony Bennett. And it didn't include me. But I'm not bitter.

It's hard for me to even imagine that kind of wealth. It would be hard for subjects of King Xerxes to imagine it too. But, on the last seven days of this exclusive feast, Xerxes threw open the doors to everyone small and great. Even the servants got a taste of the world's finest.

Just in time for some marital fireworks.

Enter the Queen.

> Queen Vashti also made a feast for the women in the royal palace which belonged to King Ahasuerus. (Esther 1:9, NKJV)

Notice where Vashti threw her soirée. "In the royal palace which belonged to King Ahasueras [Xerxes]." It's her feast, but it's still his palace.

I wonder why the Storyteller included this information. It goes without saying that the palace belongs to the king, so why include, and even emphasize, this tidbit? The way the story is told you begin to suspect that everyone and everything is just an appendage of the king. Let's watch for more of that.

The opening paragraphs offer a glimpse into unthinkable opulence. Impressive, glamorous, and powerful. If the book just ended right here, it would almost be a fairy tale ending. Happily ever after.

Why can't it just stay that way? Why can't life have fairy tale endings?

How can the bride who gushed into a microphone about finding her "soul-mate" be so soon packing her bags to move back in with her mother? No fairy tale ending there.

How can your beautiful child who loved God and was so involved in church, plunge into the dark side of life? No fairy tale ending here either. Not yet, at least.

How can your life clip along with a loving family, wonderful friends, and perfect health—when one morning you feel a small lump where no lump should be?

How can the same world, the same family, the same person be so wonderful one moment and so messed up the next?

This is the world in which we who follow Jesus must live. Fairy tale endings are in short supply.

When we just look at the surface, it's easy to be dazzled and starry-eyed.

But look out! Too often the world is not as impressive as it sometimes appears to be.

A Dangerous World

If the first scene weaves a beautiful tapestry, the second scene unravels it fast.

> On the seventh day of the feast, when King Xerxes was half drunk with wine, he told Mehuman, Biztha, Harbona, Bigtha, Abagtha, Zethar, and Carcas, the seven eunuchs who attended him, to bring Queen Vashti to him with the royal crown on her head. He wanted all the men to gaze on her beauty, for she was a very beautiful woman. (Esther 1:10,11)

My friend's mom pulled him aside at his second daughter's first birthday party and promised to leave his girls—her granddaughters—a large sum of money in her will. There was one condition, however. My friend could not tell his wife—the girls' mother—about the gift at all. It was a gift with strings attached. Beware whenever other people seek to trap you in their web of OPC.

Consider the crown King Xerxes commands Queen Vashti to wear. He gave it to her—perhaps as a wedding gift. But which was it: a loving gesture to honor his bride and queen, or another tool to stroke his own ego?

Some experts interpret the king's summons to mean that Vashti should be brought naked to his feast. I don't see that, but does it matter? He just wants to display her, the way a carmaker displays new models at car shows. He won't admit it, but Xerxes wants the queen to radiate his glory, not her own.

How do you handle OPC? Vashti runs a clinic.

A Short Course on Handling OPC

> But when they conveyed the king's order to Queen Vashti, she refused to come. This made the king furious, and he burned with anger. (Esther 1:12)

When my now teenage son was little, he was a fair incarnation of Calvin in *Calvin and Hobbes*. One Easter, we planned to take a family picture after church. J.D. has always been allergic to posing for pictures.

"J.D., come over here and we'll take our picture really fast."

His five-year-old eyes got big. He set his jaw, dug in his heels, bit his lower lip and contemplated the enormity of his decision. With tears of defiance and a grimly determined countenance, my son shook his head in a deliberate, unequivocal, slow-motion "No."

His little face said it all. He was fully aware that there would be consequences, but he stood by his choice anyway. *I will not let you get a good family picture with me. And you know what you can do with your consequences.*

I held back a laugh and was impressed by his determination, but we still got our picture: "J.D., get over here now or forget about hunting Easter eggs at Grandma's." He came. Consequences averted.

I have to believe that when Vashti said no, she knew there would be consequences. But she'd had enough. She would no longer react to him. She would set her own agenda and he would react to her.

This is a breakthrough moment.

The original Hebrew features some details that don't come out very well in any English translation. The first two times, the Author literally calls her "Vashti, the queen" (vv. 9, 11). But this time she reverses the words: "The queen, Vashti" (v. 12).

What's the difference?

The difference is between being queen in name only versus being queen in conduct. Vashti rises up to her full stature as royalty.

What will it take to handle Other People's Craziness?

Sooner or later you have to rise to your full stature and push back against crazy people.

Vashti did, triggering a chain reaction of cataclysmic events.

Many times we can't say no to our exploiters. Either we are too young, too frightened, too much in danger, or too unsure. I get that. These are times when Other People's Craziness requires extreme caution. That caution may very well save your life. Be careful. Be smart. I applaud your caution.

Be aware, however. In the long haul your caution comes with a high price tag: your dignity, your happiness, your independence, and your safety.

The day will come when you must choose. That day will be your moment to shine. That glorious moment when you refuse your exploiter's command. Just like Vashti did. When that day comes, push back hard. Fight OPC in the most righteous way you can. Leave the consequences to God. The rest of Esther shows how.

> But when they conveyed the king's order to Queen Vashti, she refused to come. This made the king furious, and he burned with anger. (Esther 1:12)

The difference between a gentleman and a bully is how he reacts when you tell him "No."

The impressive, wealthy, glamorous world turns on its ear in a matter of moments. Everything switched. The king switched from glorious monarch to peeved child. The party switched from joyous celebration to stressed-out whispering. The world switched from dazzling to deadly. And when it switched, it switched fast.

What is the Author driving at?

We live in a crazy world. You can't predict it. Today's pleasures can be tomorrow's torments. Even when it looks glamorous, our world is rotten to the core. Overly pessimistic? Perhaps, but that is the reality of Vashti's life.

It might be the reality of your life, too.

Plus, it gets worse. Not only must Vashti deal with OPC from her own husband, she now has the whole royal cabinet, staffed by snooty know-it-alls, eager to help the king solve the nightmare that he thinks Vashti has become.

A Ridiculous World

> He immediately consulted with his advisers, who knew all the Persian laws and customs, for he always asked their advice. The names of these men were Carshena, Shethar, Admatha, Tarshish, Meres, Marsena, and Memucan—seven high officials of Persia and Media. They were his closest associates and held the highest positions in the empire. "What must be done to Queen Vashti?" the king demanded. "What penalty does the law provide for a queen who refuses to obey the king's orders, properly sent through his eunuchs?" (Esther 1:13-15)

With remorseless understatement, the Author profiles an appallingly impotent king. He relates to his wife through servants. He relies on underlings to think for him. He makes a federal case out of his wife's decision. He worries excessively over image. He banks on eunuchs to do his heavy lifting (think about that).

The glorious King Xerxes has no clothes. He comes across as a nut, just like so many people you rub shoulders with every day. It's not your fault.

As you read Memucan's response in the next paragraph, make your voice get whinier, louder, and higher pitched with each increasingly ridiculous sentence.

Memucan answered the king and his princes, "Queen Vashti has wronged not only the king but also every official and citizen throughout your empire. Women everywhere will begin to despise their husbands when they learn that Queen Vashti has refused to appear before the king. Before this day is out, the wife of every one of us, your officials throughout the empire, will hear what the queen did and will start talking to their husbands the same way. There will be no end to the contempt and anger throughout your realm. So if it please the king, we suggest that you issue a written decree, a law of the Persians and Medes that cannot be revoked. It should order that Queen Vashti be forever banished from your presence and that you choose another queen more worthy than she. When this decree is published throughout your vast empire, husbands everywhere, whatever their rank, will receive proper respect from their wives!" (Esther 1:16-20)

A dad informs his teenage daughter that she can't use the car tonight. This triggers a queenly snit: "That's soooo not fair! You always do this to me! You're, like, trying to ruin my life! [Shrieking...] Why can't you ever be like Sydney's dad? He's so cool. And you're like totally mean. And, like, I'm going to lose all my friends. You're wrecking my WHOLE LIFE. I'M NEVER TALKING TO YOU AGAIN! [Door Slams... Sobbing.]" Teenage OPC: particularly virulent.

Memucan, the king's advisor, pushes Vashti's action to an illogical conclusion. He globalizes her choice and horribilizes its consequences. In the original Hebrew, he uses the word "all" five times: Vashti has wronged all the princes, and all the people, in all the king's provinces. All the women will hear about it and all the noblewomen will defy their husbands.

I'd classify this as severe Social Network OPC.

The truth is that honor cannot be forced or commanded or legislated. But that is just what insecure men and women try to do.

Sooner or later, OPC always backfires. In this case, it's sooner. What is the one thing that Vashti did not want to do? Come before the king. So how does the king's brain-trust punish her? They pass a law: You can no longer come before the king.

Okay. No problem.

> The king and his princes thought this made good sense, so he followed Memucan's counsel. He sent letters to all parts of the empire, to each province in its own script and language, proclaiming that every man should be the ruler of his home. (Esther 1:21, 22)

Verse 21 literally says that Memucan's advice "pleased the king." King Xerxes isn't in charge; his hormones are.

Because that's how the world is. People in our lives are so often clueless. Controlling. Overreacting. Hormonal. Unreasonable.

Think about the implications of this decision. Insecure men back up their domestic authority with the force of law. Women the world over drop one more rung on the social ladder, and males—many of them cruel, harsh, exploitative—have yet another weapon in their arsenal to control their wives.

There's no way this law can do any good. It cannot further love and affection in the home. It cannot bring honor to a man. It positively dishonors women. The king projects his craziness throughout the whole system. He magnifies family OPC into systemic OPC. That's the price of letting crazies run the show.

A Fallen World

The story moves from impressive to ridiculous faster than a Hollywood divorce. If the palace of Persia is a microcosm of your world, then what is the nature of your world? What are the deep truths about the society in which you live, play, work, study, raise your family, and serve God?

You live in a morally fallen world. It may be glamorous at its surface, but underneath skulks a hellish core. This fallen world is a morally broken pain machine.

You can't avoid it. You can't escape it. You can't fix it.

Even worse, the pain machine is fueled by unrelenting hostility from the Prince of Darkness, Satan himself (1 John 1:19). You live in the crosshairs of a cosmic battle, a warfare that spans the ages.

That's why bad stuff happens.

That's where OPC ultimately finds its power.

You have to deal with it. I'm so sorry.

How will you be a faithful follower of Jesus in this crazy, fallen world? Are you equipped to keep faith with God and to keep true to yourself in the face of Other People's Craziness?

𒐌𒐖𒐊𒌋𒐊𒐖

Reflections

Reflections 1: Play the game, but get ready to walk off the field.

Vashti played the game for a long time. Finally, she said, Enough! She marched off the field of play, and into the annals of history.

For some Christ-followers, society has passed the moral point of no return. To them, our larger culture is irredeemable. So they check out, like the Amish. They deal with Other People's Craziness through isolation.

Can we ever successfully isolate ourselves from the world? Should we try? What does Jesus want for his followers?

Jesus salted us into the world to season and preserve it (Matthew 5:13). We followers of Jesus belong here. We're needed. We're on a joint-mission with Jesus. Our spiritually hungry neighbors long for what we possess—even if they don't know it. We must stay in the game. Love for our God-seeking world won't let us stomp off the field in a huff.

But we can't afford to keep getting pounded either. There will come a time when you must push back. Like Vashti did. Let Xerxes keep his crown—Vashti kept her dignity. If we are ridiculed as being out of touch, or uptight, or antiquated, or quaint, so be it. Vashti walked away from the glory of an empire. She let it go for the sake of her own sanity.

What will you let go of for your sanity? What oppressor will you defy? OPC has an Achilles' heel that it doesn't want you to know about: *Other People's Craziness has no right to rule you except what you give it.* When you push back, and really mean it, OPC unhinges its jaw, releases its grip, and slithers back under its rock.

If there's a malignant case of OPC wrecking your life, get help. Talk to a women's refuge. A pastor. The police. Line up family and friends. Take care of yourself and your kids. Plan your escape. Enlist your allies.

Then go. Leave. Don't live with abuse. You weren't created to be anybody's punching bag, physically or emotionally. Dethrone your abuser. OPC has no rights to you. You belong to God.

Stop letting the crazy people tell you what's sane, okay?

FOR REFLECTION AND DISCUSSION: In Matthew 19:29, what reward does Jesus promise to those who walk off the field for his sake? Discuss or journal a time when you or someone you know dethroned an abuser.

Reflections 2: Trust God, even when you can't find him.

Where was God when the king decided to exploit Vashti? Did he whisper in her ear, "Don't worry! I'll protect you?" Did he appear in a vision? Did he comfort her in any way? No.

As far as the story goes, God wasn't in the picture at all.

Most days, he's not in the picture for me, either. At least not obviously. Evidently, God likes to hide. You can't tell how or when or even if he'll make his presence known.

Sometimes God elevates us to heights of victory; other times we go down in flames.

Sometimes he heals; other time the body weakens and dies.

Sometimes he stops the exploiter dead in his tracks; other times, the exploitation persists.

Where was God?

If Esther's first chapter reveals anything about God it is this: *There is a lot more that we do NOT know about God than we do know.* Call it the Divine Uncertainty Principle. As soon as you accept it, you will have made a huge stride forward in your struggle against OPC.

I am not trying to undercut the clear teaching of the Word of God. The Bible overflows with divine certainties. We should learn them and count on them.

But, in this world, we can never predict exactly how God will answer our prayers. We can't strong-arm him by "positive confession." We can't manipulate him by "name it and claim it." We can't see all the ins and outs of his intricate plan.

"Even when we cannot see God's hand, we can still trust his heart" (Charles H. Spurgeon).

That's what makes faith so pleasing to God. If you could see the end of your story, you wouldn't need day-by-day faith. It is our very inability to see God's presence that makes faith so precious. Every time you stretch forth that mostly intimidated foot of yours and plant it shakily into uncharted territory, God is pleased. You may lose the world's crown, but rejoice: you'll gain God's.

Your job is faith; God's job is outcomes.

Plus, you'll gain rewards in heaven that will one day make you say, "It was worth it all" (2 Corinthians 4:17).

FOR REFLECTION AND DISCUSSION: What does Isaiah 55:8, 9 say about the Divine Uncertainty Principle? Discuss or journal a recent bout of doubts you've had about God.

CHAPTER 4

OPC and Grace

TONIGHT, I WILL LOSE MY VIRGINITY. I never imagined it this way. Why, God?

The echoes of her footsteps fill the chilly hall. She hazards a glance at the ornate door and quickly looks away. What monster lurks behind? She resumes pacing.

I can do this. I have no choice. She chokes down a primal dread. Resistance is futile. Running is impossible. She wrings her hands without realizing.

In a few moments, when that massive door swings open, her whole life will be at stake. It will be the audition of a lifetime. Most women would give anything for it. But not her. She doesn't want it. She's never wanted it.

Just get it over with! What's taking so long?

Her fingers clench and unclench. Acid burns her throat. She fights back an urge to vomit. She already feels violated.

Footsteps! Adrenaline surges through her system. Her eyes close, desperate to blot out reality.

A flurry of activity among the staff. False smiles. Insincere welcomes.

She wills her face to smile. Her lungs to fill. Her hands to stop shaking. She smoothes her shimmering gown. Only the most determined onlooker can now detect the resentment that engulfs her. Her training has served her well. She radiates composure.

The attendant unlatches the door. It swings open silently. She catches a whiff of cologne. She hears trickling water and soothing music. The moment is surreal, as if she watches from afar.

A voice calls her name. Not the one her mother gave her, the name from her all too brief childhood—but the name *he* gave her.

Tonight, I will lose my virginity. I never pictured it this way.

She gasps when she sees him.

Tall, muscular, naked from the waist up. His head, chest and body are shaved smooth except for a neatly trimmed beard. His lips neither smile nor frown. He eyes her from head to foot to head, like a buyer at the stockyards. He circles her partway and sniffs.

Swallowing hard, she locks eyes with him, parts her lips, tilts her chin upward, and steps forward.

Her silent prayer: *Lord, make him gentle.*

𒐉 𒀭 𒈫 𒐏 𒐉 𒐋

It's sad to imagine that the new Queen of the known world—Vashti's successor—would be selected based on one night's performance in bed. But that is exactly what happens in the crazy world of Esther 2.

But after Xerxes' anger had cooled, he began thinking about Vashti and what she had done and the decree he had made. So his attendants suggested, "Let us search the empire to find beautiful young virgins for the king. Let the king appoint agents in each province to bring these beautiful young women into the royal harem at Susa. Hegai, the eunuch in charge, will see that they are all given beauty treatments. After that, the young woman who pleases you most will be made queen instead of Vashti." This advice was very appealing to the king, so he put the plan into effect immediately. (Esther 2:1-4)

When my kids were little, they invented a fictional troublemaker to blame when they did something wrong. They blamed "Mr. Nobody." After an extremely chaotic playtime, J.D. plopped down on the sofa and surveyed the disaster area formerly known as our family room. Toys littered the furniture. The rug was a minefield of cars, stuffed animals, rifles, and megablocks. My son laid back, crossed his legs, and observed, "Mr. Nobody sure gets around."

Yes he does, son.

Can you ever remember a time when some nut-job actually took total responsibility for his or her lunacy? OPC perpetrators blame their carnage on anybody but themselves.

Mr. Nobody caused King Xerxes' newfound loneliness. Xerxes remembered, "what *she* had done." It was her fault. And he remembered the law "that had been decreed against her" (literal translation). A passive voice verb—as if the law to banish Vashti had magically written itself.

For the second time, the king makes a federal case out of a problem with women. Also for the second time, the king lets other people solve his problems. He accepts their solution and sends forth his officers "to gather" beautiful women from all over his realm. Gather them. Like you would gather dirty clothes for a load of laundry or tools after you've finished repairing the car. What if they don't want to be gathered?

Irrelevant.

A CIA dossier of the king might look like this: King Xerxes is a passive, self-pitying, blame-shifting, immature weakling who solves his problems by exploiting others—especially the weak and vulnerable. But he throws an awesome party.

He has the position of king, but the heart of a victim. Contrast the king's profile to that of Mordecai and Esther.

The Soul of Royalty

Now at the fortress of Susa there was a certain Jew named Mordecai son of Jair. He was from the tribe of Benjamin and was a descendant of Kish and Shimei. His family had been exiled from Jerusalem to Babylon by King Nebuchadnezzar, along with King Jehoiachin of Judah and many others. This man had a beautiful and lovely young cousin, Hadassah, who was also called Esther. When her father and mother had died, Mordecai adopted her into his family and raised her as his own daughter. (Esther 2:5-7)

The first factoid in Mordecai's profile is that he is a third-generation exile from his homeland. Verse 6 emphasizes this four times in the original Hebrew, so you won't miss it. Why? Because you're supposed to view Mordecai as a bona fide qualifier for the Victim T-shirt.

Same with Esther. I get nervous just reading about her. She was born in exile and then her parents died. So you're introduced to an orphan who is also a refugee. Picture a weeping child, toddling down a dirt road, crying for her mommy and daddy, surrounded by uncaring strangers who speak a foreign tongue. That's Esther. In a very real way, Esther is also a bona fide victim.

Now, however, for the first time, the Author sounds a note of grace. Mordecai "adopted" Esther. The Hebrew word is "amen." The root indicates firmness or certainty, as in strong arms upholding a helpless infant. Mordecai is a solid rock in Esther's shaky world.

Don't forget that he, too, is a victim. If anybody could shrug his shoulders and say, "I can't help her—my life is in shambles. I'm a [sniff] victim!" it was Mordecai. "Let Mr. Nobody help her."

But Mordecai had a different spirit.

Why? Because the heartbreaks of life do not exempt you from a life of love and service to others. OPC doesn't define you. It doesn't limit the borders of your life. It has no power except what you give it. Mordecai survived it. You can too.

No matter how crazy your world becomes, you are never fated to a wretched, second-rate existence. No amount of Other People's Craziness can determine your destiny. You can choose a destiny besides the one the crazies have in mind for you.

King Xerxes has the position of power, but the heart of a victim.

Mordecai has the position of victim, but the heart of a king.

Mordecai or Xerxes: which one would be a more accurate poster child for your life?

Let's watch as the hero of the story sinks neck deep into a vat of toxic OPC and emerges a glorious queen—bloodied, but unbowed.

> As a result of the king's decree, Esther, along with many other young women, was brought to the king's harem at the fortress of Susa and placed in Hegai's care. (Esther 2:8)

This is a sex competition. The future queen of the known world will be decided by her one-night performance in bed with the king. Winner take all.

What kind of world is this? It's a crazy, dangerous, uncertain world

In the Empire of Persia, the sexual lives of subjects belonged to the king: both males and females. An ancient historian named Herodotus tells us that every year King Xerxes forcibly extracted five hundred boys from Babylon. These boys were castrated and trained to guard his harem.

The morality or immorality of Esther having sex with the king is not the point here. She had to. She had no choice.

You might have had no choice either, sexually speaking. An older neighbor, a drunken father, a perverted mother, an exploitative teacher, or a depraved priest. No statistics can convey the grief of stolen innocence. I'm so sad with you. Angry too. It's not your fault.

But it's not the last chapter in your life either. You get to write the rest of the story.

Grace in the Harem

Hegai was very impressed with Esther and treated her kindly. He quickly ordered a special menu for her and provided her with beauty treatments. He also assigned her seven maids specially chosen from the king's palace, and he moved her and her maids into the best place in the harem. (Esther 2:9)

You'll find a handful of people in the Bible who had a knack for thriving in terrible situations. A man named Joseph was attacked by his brothers—talk about family OPC—and found himself a slave on his way to Egypt. Yet he ended up running a vast estate for his wealthy master. Later, after being viciously betrayed, Joseph ran the prison his master sent him to. Ultimately he ran the empire of Egypt, second only to Pharaoh. No matter how much life pounded him, Joseph pounded back.

Or consider Daniel. Taken hostage in his teen years, Daniel successfully resisted Babylonian brainwashing and religious indoctrination. Yet the Babylonian king promoted him to chief of staff. Later he promoted Daniel again to run the entire empire of Babylon. Like Joseph, Daniel possessed an almost mystical ability to flourish in the bleakest situations.

Looks like Esther might have that ability too.

When I read their stories, I'm tempted to dismiss them as either insanely lucky or ultra-spiritual. Either judgment allows me to write them off as virtually irrelevant to my life. I assume I'll never be as lucky or as spiritual as them, so I toss their stories on the mental trash heap with the other impractical stuff in my life.

But what if God tells their stories to communicate abiding principles that *anybody* can use—even the spiritually remedial and tragically unlucky? What if the Bible includes the stories of Joseph and Daniel and Esther as real-life clinics on dealing with OPC? And what if their successes resulted from faithfulness to abiding principles instead of luck or ultra-spirituality? If they could master the art of dealing with OPC, maybe we can too.

For some reason, Esther stood out among the virginal recruits. She was given the finest menu, the best beauty treatments, the most glamorous housing, and the most experienced servants.

Why Esther?

Verse 9 says that the king's guard treated her "kindly." Other Bibles use the word "favor". The original Hebrew literally says that Esther "found grace in his sight." (The Hebrew word is spelled *hesed*. Lock that in the memory banks. We'll see it again).

What does it mean?

It means that OPC has met its match. God has woven a force into your life to counteract the power of OPC. That force is called *grace*.

What is grace? Grace is the power of God, churning out consistent, extravagant, undeserved kindness for you—kindness that always comes at God's expense. We'll run into more grace later. In this case, grace gave Esther the power to rise above OPC.

You might have detected some sleight of hand here: I inserted God into Esther's story though the Author hasn't mentioned him yet. Guilty as charged. I confess that I'm racing ahead of the story theologically, but let me plead my case.

You'll find about fifty examples in the Bible in which somebody finds grace (*hesed* or similar terms) in somebody else's sight. Noah found grace in God's sight (Genesis 6:8). So did Moses (Exodus 33:12) and Mary, the mother of Jesus (Luke 1:30).

Others found grace in human eyes, like Joseph before his master (Genesis 39:4) and Ruth before Boaz (Ruth 2:2).

Esther found grace in Hegai's sight. So how do I justify inserting God into the equation?

A thorough investigation of all these cases of grace (or of favor, mercy, lovingkindness, or kindness—depending on your Bible translation) leads you to conclude that all grace originates in God, though he often uses humans to deploy it.

So when the Bible says that Esther "found grace" in the eyes of a pagan, Persian eunuch, it's fair to conclude that God was using him as a channel of divine grace.

And divine grace possesses an inherent power to knock out OPC.

Whatever craziness Esther faces, she doesn't face it alone. An Unseen Hand supplies grace, even in her most exploitative, disorienting, OPC-ish situation. Even in a bedroom she'd rather not be in. Grace is there for her.

It's there for you too. That same Unseen Hand will supply OPC-crushing grace to you. Even if your ex's latest halitosis-afflicted boyfriend wants to be your good buddy. Even if your daughter hooks up with the surfer-dude from hell who dropped out of college to tramp the world's beaches for the perfect wave. Even if eunuchs are suddenly placed in charge of you in a foreign king's harem. God's grace is there.

Identity Crisis

Esther had not told anyone of her nationality and family background, for Mordecai had told her not to. Every day Mordecai would take a walk near the courtyard of the harem to ask about Esther and to find out what was happening to her. (Esther 2:10, 11)

Though I was not shy about being a Christian, I was painfully shy about God's inner insistence that I become a pastor. I wanted nothing to do with pastor-hood. I knew from age eight that God called me into ministry. I didn't hear a spooky, audible voice. I simply felt an inner realization that never went away.

But I thought that pastors were dorky, and that, if I told my friends I was going to become one, I would lose my "totally-cool" status.

Okay, I may be embellishing my status a little, but that's beside the point.

Because I let peer pressure and its bad OPC-juju deform my identity, I began to suffer a crisis. Who am I? Why am I here? Where should I go to college? These questions plagued me. So, though I finished high school near the top of my class, my college career was a mess. I tried out eight different majors in three different colleges and wasted a lot of money and time along the way.

I took a job as a produce clerk in a grocery store instead. A noble profession, but not the one I had been created for. I was frustrated.

Why?

Because I wouldn't own up to my God-given identity. I didn't want anybody to know the real me: the guy that sincerely wanted to please God as a pastor, but dreaded the backlash from my peers.

OPC always strikes at the heart of your identity. Esther could not reveal her true self: a Jew, a covenant-child of God. That information was classified. Think of the awkward situations her secret would create:

HULDAH: Hey, Esther, you've got to try this lobster! It's yummy—dip it in the butter. It's to die for! [Slurp!]

ESTHER'S CONSCIENCE: *Thou shalt not eat shellfish— it's not kosher.*

ESTHER: Uhhh, no thanks, I'm watching my weight. Big day's coming, you know. Gotta look good for the king.

HULDAH: Yeah, I understand. Too bad. But, hey, just skip the butter! It's still delicious. Protein makes your skin glow. You're doing Atkins, right? Here, have a taste.

ESTHER'S CONSCIENCE: *You told your cousin, Mordecai, that you'd keep your Jewishness a secret.*

ESTHER: Well, umm—I can't. Uhhh. No thanks.

HULDAH: Really? C'mon it's scrumptious, isn't it girls?

GIRLS: Omigosh! Awesome!

HULDAH: Speaking of scrumptious, how about that Zebag! He's got those cute dimples, he can sing, and, yow! can he cook! [Long sigh.] Too bad he's a eunuch. A waste of manhood. Esther, you're always so picky! Here, squeeze a lemon on it. Just a little nibble. Say ahh...

ESTHER: Ummm... Well... I can't... I'm... uhh... allergic to shellfish! That's it. Yes! I'm allergic!

I don't blame Esther one bit. She had to dodge. Maybe her life depended on it. I'm not about to condemn anybody who faces OPC, especially deadly dangerous OPC like Esther. She's a survivor. Like me to some degree. Like you, too. There are times to just be wise and bide your time.

Still, there's a price to pay. Until you allow your true identity to shine, consider yourself under the thumb of OPC, at least a little. It wasn't until I finally unleashed my inner pastor that I felt honest, authentic, and real.

One day, I just did it. Consciously, deliberately, for no reason other than I was finally willing. I literally prayed, "Okay God. I'll do this pastor thing." I immediately enrolled in my third college and actually earned a degree.

I even told people I was studying to be a pastor.

Free at last!

OPC will gnaw at your identity like a vulture on road kill.

Which makes me wonder: if Esther found grace in Hegai's eyes, and was given all the best treatments, why wasn't that grace sufficient for her to be her real self? Why still bury such a huge enchilada as her identity? Maybe the grace wasn't enough?

My theory is that the Author knows that Esther found grace; the readers know that Esther found grace. Everybody knows that Esther found grace, except Esther. We know more than she does. She's still slogging through her OPC swamp all alone (she thinks). It will take a few chapters before the grace she's received dawns on her.

Which makes me wonder something else: how much grace has God lavished on me that I haven't noticed yet?

Pause and consider.

Final Exams

Before each young woman was taken to the king's bed, she was given the prescribed twelve months of beauty treatments—six months with oil of myrrh, followed by six months with special perfumes and ointments. When the time came for her to go in to the king, she was given her choice of whatever clothing or jewelry she wanted to enhance her beauty. That evening she was taken to the king's private rooms, and the next morning she was brought to the second harem, where the king's wives lived. There she would be under the care of Shaashgaz, another of the king's eunuchs. She would live there for the rest of her life, never going to the king again unless he had especially enjoyed her and requested her by name. (Esther 2:11-14)

How much stress did you feel before final exams? Multiply that a bit and you might begin to empathize with Esther. Except, her final exam included giving up her virginity in a sexual romp that would be graded by a man who enjoyed the eager pleasures of an exotic woman from a different country every night. Any class rank less than valedictorian relegated her to a second-class life in the harem for castaways until death do us part.

But no pressure.

Finally, Esther's day arrives. Heart pounding, mind racing, palms sweating, Esther stands before the private chamber of the mightiest ruler on earth. Her name is called. The door swings open...

> When it was Esther's turn to go to the king, she accepted the advice of Hegai, the eunuch in charge of the harem. She asked for nothing except what he suggested, and she was admired by everyone who saw her. When Esther was taken to King Xerxes at the royal palace in early winter of the seventh year of his reign, the king loved her more than any of the other young women. He was so delighted with her that he set the royal crown on her head and declared her queen instead of Vashti. To celebrate the occasion, he gave a banquet in Esther's honor for all his princes and servants, giving generous gifts to everyone and declaring a public festival for the provinces. Even after all the young women had been transferred to the second harem and Mordecai had become a palace official, Esther continued to keep her nationality and family background a secret. She was still following Mordecai's orders, just as she did when she was living in his home. (Esther 2:15-20)

One of my pastor friends, Andy, confessed, "Bill, whenever my wife and I visited church friends, I pre-briefed her. I told her what to say and what not to say. I told her who to talk to and who not to talk to. I told her what to wear. I didn't want her to spoil my image."

Andy used to pastor a megachurch.

He also used to be married.

Can you detect some of Xerxes' spirit in Andy? Each wanted to control his world. To orchestrate and define it. Each wanted to dominate the people in his life. Andy, like Xerxes, believed that control was the secret of happiness.

We have a technical term for this belief: craziness.

The good news is that Esther wins the king's heart and ascends to the throne of Persia.

The bad news is that Esther wins the king's heart and ascends to the throne of Persia.

Don't mistake Esther's victory for a fairy-tale ending. It is not. Esther still serves the king's pleasure. She still hides her true identity. She still plays by the OPC rules. Esther's story is not "happily ever after."

And my hunch is that neither is yours, at least not yet. So, does that mean you give up? That you have a right to be bitter and angry?

Heck yes! Let's go on strike, doggone it. I'll make the pickets. You type up the press release. I'll start a petition. I'm sick of it. Outraged! I want my happy ending, and I want it right now. I demand my rights. Are you with me?

Hello?

You're right. There's a better way. The Author just about whacked us over the head with grace three more times (literal translations from the Hebrew):

- Verse 15: Esther found grace [*hen*—compassionate grace]
- Verse 17: Esther found grace [*hen*—compassionate grace]
- Verse 17: and grace [*hesed*—unmerited grace]

What is God saying?

He's practically shouting, DON'T FORGET THE GRACE-FACTOR. Grace is this crazy world's great equalizer. The Author adds some stars to the grace constellation by using two different Hebrew words. The first word emphasizes the compassionate tenderness of grace (the Hebrew word *hen*—pronounced *hayn*—in v. 15, and the first term in v. 17). The second word emphasizes the unmerited loyalty of grace—this is *hesed*, which we met in v. 9.

Hebrew technicalities aside, Esther's success pits OPC versus Grace, and Grace wins by a knockout. With all this grace-stuff, the Author may be setting up a major lesson about OPC: that rising above OPC somehow hinges on grace. We'll have to see.

A Strange Ending

One day as Mordecai was on duty at the palace, two of the king's eunuchs, Bigthana and Teresh—who were guards at the door of the king's private quarters—became angry at King Xerxes and plotted to assassinate him. But Mordecai heard about the plot and passed the information on to Queen Esther. She then told the king about it and gave Mordecai credit for the report. When an investigation was made and Mordecai's story was found to be true, the two men were hanged on a gallows. This was all duly recorded in The Book of the History of King Xerxes' Reign. (Esther 2:21-23)

As a finale to the chapter, this paragraph sticks out like a Baptist in a mosh pit. But don't sidestep it: the moves here set up some fancy footwork later.

Here is the plot so far:

Point A—a disgruntled Queen thumbs her nose at her Royal Pain in the OPC, so that...

Point B—an orphaned refugee, reared by a relative in a foreign land succeeds her, thus being in perfect position...

Point Z—to indirectly save King Xerxes' life.

How did the story get from A to Z?

Only through an implausible series of events that would make you put down any other novel by the end of the second chapter.

The Author invites her readers to marvel at the links in a causal chain: 1. Vashti refused the king's command, leading to: 2. An international beauty contest, which was preceded by: 3. The death of Esther's parents, leading to: 4. Mordecai's adoption of her, discovering that: 5. Esther is quite a beauty, thus merging her story with Xerxes', leading to: 6. Esther's grace-filled selection by Xerxes as his latest bride, enabling her to: 7. Promote cousin Mordecai to a government sinecure, so that: 8. He just happened to overhear an assassination plot, and: 9. Squealed on the would-be murderers, thus: 10. Saving the king's royal life.

Break any link in the chain, and King Xerxes is history—prematurely.

So what?

Maybe life, and all its OPC, is less random than we imagine. Though we may not see it, events happen for a reason. Even though Xerxes possesses unlimited power, he still is not the master of his destiny. Were it not for the gracious intervention of an Unseen Hand through Mordecai, he'd be dead. The king is not in control, and the tension in the story is that neither he nor the other crazies of planet earth realize it yet.

𒐀𒐀𒐀𒐀𒐀𒐀

Reflections

Reflections 1: No matter how hard you try to control your world, your life still depends on the One who holds the world in the palm of his hand.

Theology experts have a word for God's shepherding of the universe: Providence. Providence means that God arranges the details of the world to bring about his own purposes and goals. He governs all things, so that not even one sub-atomic particle wiggles without his knowledge and permission.

He is infinite God. We are finite humans. To orchestrate even one day of our lives is harder than controlling the waves of the sea. We can't do it. We might make a ripple here or there, but for God it's a piece of cake. Even the waves march at God's command.

Does this mean that we are pawns? Not at all. We are royalty and we have free will—so much that God calls it "dominion" and tells us to go forth and exercise it (Genesis 1:28). God, in his providence, easily factors in our choices and dominion.

We believe in providence, not luck, not karma, not chance, not "what will be will be." God wanted Esther where she was so he could keep Xerxes where he was so God could accomplish stuff we have no clue about.

Xerxes' life was in the palm of an Unseen Hand. Makes you wonder who else's life is in that hand.

FOR REFLECTION AND DISCUSSION: How does Romans 8:28 help you understand Providence? Discuss or journal a time when an Unseen Hand orchestrated events beyond your control.

Reflections 2: Our lives will always have uncertainty.

Again the Storyteller creates this feeling by omission. She doesn't mention God at all for two whole chapters, spanning at least a year's time. Can you relate?

Why did God let the Jews get exiled? Why did Esther's parents both die? Why did a man like Xerxes take the throne? Lots of whys.

Which God is content to leave unanswered. If Esther's parents hadn't died, the king would have been killed and the two are connected on a level our little minds can't fathom.

If God were so simple that our minds could understand him, he'd be so simple that he wouldn't be God.

FOR REFLECTION AND DISCUSSION: According to Deuteronomy 29:29, what belongs to us and what belongs to God? Discuss or journal how you typically react when you feel uncertain about God and his ways in your life.

Reflections 3: Grace has more power to uphold you than OPC has power to degrade you.

Even if the giant pain machine of earth chews you up, God, in his providence, supplies what you need. If God can supply grace to Esther from Hegai, keeper of the king's harem, and if he can supply grace to Esther from Xerxes, a pagan, self-serving king, then he can supply grace to you.

We can thunder against heaven with our anger, and pester God and our own hearts with questions about why OPC happens, but God seems unwilling to answer. He even seems unwilling to acknowledge that he heard the question.

The fact is that God is so immense, so vast, and so unsearchable, that even after eternity rolls on, we will only be scratching the surface of his nature and his ways.

But we do know that our truest, highest, royalty lies in our willingness to take his hand and have faith. Where does that leave us? Trusting like children, finding his grace, and living a great adventure called life. Whatever wounds OPC might inflict, grace stands ready to get you through it, and God stands ready to make it worth it all. You just have to believe.

FOR REFLECTION AND DISCUSSION: From 1 Corinthians 10:13, identify 2 or 3 ways that God's grace helps you through tough times. Discuss or journal how much you really believe what God is saying in this verse.

CHAPTER 5

OPC and Evil

IT'S TIME TO MEET ONE OF THE MOST CONNIVING, manipulative, evil men in the whole Bible. His name is Haman. And he hatches a plan to exterminate the Jews.

> Some time later, King Xerxes promoted Haman son of Hammedatha the Agagite to prime minister, making him the most powerful official in the empire next to the king himself. (Esther 3:1)

Picture a storyteller at a late night campfire, introducing Haman to a bunch of kids. Haman was an Agagite, and this would make the kids around the campfire gasp. Being an Agagite made him an Amalekite.

Which probably means nothing to you. But the original readers of this book might have broken into a cold sweat. The Amalekites were historic enemies of the Jews. They wanted to wipe Israel off the map. Now, one of their tribe ascends to the king's right hand.

Remember, we're letting the Persian throne room represent your world and every world. It has already shown itself to be a crazy, ridiculous, dangerous place. Now its evil streak is showing. Can God's people keep faith with him, and can we still experience his blessing, even when we're stuck under the thumb of other people's evil?

How do you respond to the Hamans of the world today?

> All the king's officials would bow down before Haman to show him respect whenever he passed by, for so the king had commanded. But Mordecai refused to bow down or show him respect. Then the palace officials at the king's gate asked Mordecai, "Why are you disobeying the king's command?" They spoke to him day after day, but still he refused to comply with the order. So they spoke to Haman about this to see if he would tolerate Mordecai's conduct, since Mordecai had told them he was a Jew. (Esther 3:2-4)

Water running downhill takes the path of least resistance. Massive canyons dot the landscape because of this. Even the rainwater that runs alongside my driveway gives me headaches as it erodes little ditches and washes dirt onto the pavement. The path of least resistance controls the shape of our natural world.

It controls the shape of our moral world, too. Most counselors would tell Mordecai to bow to Haman and not make waves. Take the path of least resistance! Most friends would tell Vashti to come before the king and just twirl around a few times. Humor him. Pacify him. But Mordecai and Vashti testify that, when evil runs its downhill course, somebody has to become the immoveable object that blocks its seemingly irresistible force.

Which most of us are willing to do, in theory, until we count the cost.

Mordecai, like Vashti, accepted the cost.

Nobody knows it yet, but he is the new Queen's cousin/foster-father. Through her influence, he enjoys an important post in Xerxes' palace. He is a good guy. And he is a Jew who can't stomach bowing to an Amalekite.

I can almost hear Mordecai's friends begging him, "Why make your life harder than it needs to be? Mordecai, just bow. Pleeeeeease. Bow already. It's no big deal. Everybody's doing it. It will make your life so easy. Just bow. You can bow on the outside without meaning it on the inside."

Mordecai didn't listen to those voices.

Thank God! Because Mordecai illustrates lesson one in Haman's School of Evil: *The more you bow to other people's craziness, the more craziness you'll attract.*

Every time you cave in to OPC, you're only asking for more. More evil. More manipulation. More indignity. You think you're playing nice. You think you'll make your abuser feel better about himself. You think you'll sweep the evil under the rug.

And you might, for a while. But under that rug, it will fester, double in strength, and come after you with more ferocity than before. If you're in an abusive home, you know what I'm talking about, even though you might not be ready to do anything about it yet.

The crazy people around you have an appetite that you will never satisfy, no matter how low you bow.

Mordecai knew that bowing to Haman meant bowing to evil, and would only attract more OPC in the future. So he refused to bow. Would he regret it?

> When Haman saw that Mordecai would not bow down or show him respect, he was filled with rage. So he decided it was not enough to lay hands on Mordecai alone. Since he had learned that Mordecai was a Jew, he decided to destroy all the Jews throughout the entire empire of Xerxes. (Esther 3:5,6)

HIM (yelling): "Don't you ever do that to me again! When I tell you to come here, you do it now. Right away! Don't you ever make me wait for you again, or you've had it. Do you understand me? I said DO YOU UNDERSTAND ME? Get over here right now, shut up and listen!"

ME: a scrawny seventeen-year-old clerk in a busy photofinishing store.

HIM: my hefty boss, Don, chewing me out at the top of his lungs.

THE SETTING: A store crammed with dozens of impatient customers—most of them professional photographers—waiting for us to call their number on a wet, snowy Chicago evening. Eight or nine clerks like me worked behind a long glass counter, handing finished enlargements to customers and collecting their money. I was juggling two customers on the phone and one in the store. Don summoned me. I told him I'd be with him in a minute.

That was a big mistake.

Every head in the store turned as Don chewed me out till his middle-aged, blotchy face glowed red and my teenage eyes welled with tears.

He was the meanest boss I've ever worked for. Don generated his own climate: a swell of uneasiness went before him and waves of unhappiness rolled behind him. His underlings stayed out of his way. I stood there and just took it.

When bloated pride meets nervous insecurity you get a self-absorbed brat bent on vengeance. When you toss in virtually unlimited power, you get a tyrant bent on genocide. You get Haman.

Or Don.

There's probably a Haman or two in your life. Whether it's a cruel kid in the lunchroom, a scheming in-law, or a fellow student pressuring you into illicit drugs or sex. It might be a church-person bent on gaining control. Or your buddies who treat their wives like garbage. Maybe you have a whole flock of tormentors at school, work, or home.

The spirit of Haman is alive and well. That's because the human heart is fertile soil for evil. It is, in fact, the wellspring of evil. The Bible asks, "What is causing the quarrels and fights among you? Isn't it the whole army of evil desires at war within you?" (James 4:1). And, "The heart is more deceitful than all else and is desperately sick; / Who can understand it?" (Jeremiah 17:9).

Whether you face cruel bullies at school, explosive bosses at work, or genocidal maniacs strutting the halls of power, the origin of evil is the same: a morally broken, spiritually lost heart that has dug in its heels against God. No wonder OPC is pandemic!

Lesson two in Haman's School of Evil is this: *the source of evil is the morally fallen human heart.* Lesson three will show how an evil heart brings its nefarious plans to fruition.

The Method of Evil

So in the month of April, during the twelfth year of King Xerxes' reign, lots were cast (the lots were called purim) to determine the best day and month to take action. And the day selected was March 7, nearly a year later. Then Haman approached King Xerxes and said, "There is a certain race of people scattered through all the provinces of your empire. Their laws are different from those of any other nation, and they refuse to obey even the laws of the king. So it is not in the king's interest to let them live. If it please Your Majesty, issue a decree that they be destroyed, and I will give 375 tons of silver to the government administrators so they can put it into the royal treasury." (Esther 3:7-9)

Think of it—the fate of millions of people lies in the hands of an insecure, evil, little man, who selects the date for their slaughter by rolling dice. What can you say about a man who can plot genocide so casually? What can you say about teenage boys who can publicly humiliate a girl or mean girls who can reduce a classmate to tears? Or a middle-aged boss who'll rip apart a teenage kid in front of a store full of customers?

Haman's speech stands as a masterpiece of manipulation. Notice how he spins kernels of truth into a web of lies:

"There is a certain race of people scattered and dispersed among your kingdom..." That's true.

"Their laws are different from those of any other people..." That's true too.

"And they refuse to obey even the law of the king..." The spin starts here. By and large the Jews did keep the king's law. The only exception Haman can point to is Mordecai, and the only law he broke was the king's command to bow before His Royal Punk-ness, Haman.

Haman distorts the truth and generates a false conclusion. This is the method of evil. *It exaggerates a partial truth into a gigantic lie and, from the lie, justifies its despicable conclusions.*

Some boys at my high school used this maneuver when they howled at a girl because they decided she was ugly.

Partial truth: She doesn't fit the profile of what we think a pretty high-school girl should look like.

Gigantic lie: She's ugly.

Despicable conclusion: We get to torment her, and there's nothing wrong with it.

See the pattern? My boss, Don, used the method of evil against me.

Partial truth: You didn't come to my office the instant I called you.

70

Gigantic lie: You're a bad employee and you're ruining my life.

Despicable conclusion: I get to publicly humiliate you.

Lucifer, the father of lies, perfected the method of evil in the Garden of Eden.

Partial truth: Didn't God say you can eat every fruit in the garden?

Gigantic lie: He's being inconsistent. Shouldn't "every" mean "every?" He must be holding back something from you.

Despicable conclusion: It wouldn't be wrong to eat this fruit; it would, in fact, be wrong not to.

There will always be a Haman next door, down the block, across the office, the classroom, the ocean. So if you want to live, and if you want to thrive surrounded by OPC, you have to learn how to face evil. Not how to hide from it, gloss over it, or excuse it. You have to face it, live surrounded by it, and not lose your soul. That was the challenge for Mordecai, Esther, and now all the Jews. That is the challenge for every follower of Jesus. We have to know how to face evil.

But we need to understand its method first. Haman's method is simple: start with a partial truth, twist it into a big lie, and draw a despicable conclusion.

It's the partial truth that hooks mindless drones into the gigantic lie and despicable conclusion. It's partial because it's spin. It's partial because it's not the whole truth—relevant data are slyly omitted. It's partial because it's just true enough to persuade the uncritical thinker (i.e., the vast majority). It's partial because it's framed in a way to justify something horrible. It's partial because it plays on emotion, and suggests a threat that doesn't exist.

It's the partial truth that incites the mob, and wakes up the darkest corners of the soul.

And to what end? What will Haman's plot achieve? What is the goal of evil?

> The king agreed, confirming his decision by removing his signet ring from his finger and giving it to Haman son of Hammedatha the Agagite—the enemy of the Jews. "Keep the money," the king told Haman, "but go ahead and do as you like with these people." On April 17 Haman called in the king's secretaries and dictated letters to the princes, the governors of the respective provinces, and the local officials of each province in their own scripts and languages. These letters were signed in the name of King Xerxes, sealed with his ring, and sent by messengers into all the provinces of the empire. The letters decreed that all Jews—young and old, including women and children—must be killed, slaughtered, and annihilated on a single day. This was scheduled to happen nearly a year later on March 7. The property of the Jews would be given to those who killed them. A copy of this decree was to be issued in every province and made known to all the people, so that they would be ready to do their duty on the appointed day. (Esther 3:10-14)

I can just imagine the weakling king bobbing his head as Haman makes his case. Haman casually suggests slaughtering hundreds of thousands of men, women, and (specifically) children, with the same tone of voice in which he'd order French fries off a menu.

The creepiest part for me is that Haman didn't think he was being evil. A little vindictive, maybe. A little vengeful, maybe. Exaggerating the truth. Probably. But evil? No. He was purging evil, not doing it. Mordecai was the evil-doer, so noble Haman crusaded for a righteous cause.

That's the scary part.

Compounding the creepiness, Haman bit his own bait. He offered to donate 375 tons of silver to the cause of Jewish extermination. People sacrifice for what they believe in. The human soul is fertile soil for evil; it latches onto evil like a bass lunges at a spinner bait. Only later does it feel the sharp sting of the deadly hook, though "it looked like a good idea at the time."

In a dramatic moment, the king removes his signet ring. This is the ring of authority. The ring of power. He hands it to the Diabolical Mastermind of Evil. For one solid month, with that ring in hand, Evil-personified ruled the realm.

This is what happens whenever a person in power refuses to shut down evil. Whether the evil seeps from a boss, mom, dad, pastor, teacher, student leader, businessperson, or friend, or whether it gushes from a politician, monarch, or Supreme Court Justice.

Somebody's got to push back, but nobody did.

Everybody caved in to Haman. They caved in to evil. They all bowed. They all paid homage. They all wimped out. Even the king. Everybody.

Except Mordecai.

And now, by sticking to his principles, he has unleashed a homicidal maniac upon his whole people. Was it worth it? Don't answer yet.

> At the king's command, the decree went out by the swiftest messengers, and it was proclaimed in the fortress of Susa. Then the king and Haman sat down to drink, but the city of Susa fell into confusion. (Esther 3:15)

Lesson one: *The more you bow to other people's craziness, the more craziness you'll attract.*

Lesson two: *The source of evil is the morally depraved human heart.*

Lesson three: *The method of evil is to spin partial truths into big lies and then draw despicable conclusions.*

Now, lesson four: the goal of evil—but first a story.

Some time ago I attended a pastors' conference with a famous speaker. Several years earlier, this famous speaker had been my main professor for my doctoral degree. I had taken many classes with him, and he liked me. He even told me so.

He sat me down one day and asked me if I'd do him a favor. "Depends on what it is," I said.

"My wife and I really like you, Bill, and we'd like you to date our daughter." My ears glowed red and hot. I couldn't see them, but I could sure feel them. A trickle of sweat rolled down my back. For the record, this was long before I met my wife.

Let's think about this. I am a single man, earning a doctorate, from a world-renown teacher and author, who has just asked me to date his daughter, sight unseen. Uh-huh.

I asked for a day to think about it. Then I told a couple of guys in the class. A dumb move.

Two days later, our class took a bus trip, and my fellow students—grown up, ostensibly mature, seminary doctoral students—hollered, "Hey Bill! Are you going to make out with teacher's daughter on the back of the bus?" My ears glowed again.

Sidebar: we pastoral types are not as exalted as most people think.

But that's not the real story. I told that part of it just to show you how close I was to the ecclesiastical "big time." Many years went by—and no, I didn't date his daughter—but I finished my degree, and lost contact with my professor. Then I heard he was speaking nearby at a conference. Hundreds of pastors and leaders gathered to hear him. At the conference, I wanted my fellow pastors to personally see that I was a friend of this Very Important Person.

So I pushed my way to the front of a crowd, stuck out my hand as the professor whisked by, and said, "Hi Doctor So-and-so. It's nice to see you." I expected him to cry out my name, give me a big hug, pat me on the back, and invite me to have coffee with him. So, there I stood with a big, dumb smile on my face, and my unreturned handshake hanging midair.

He looked at me. He smiled, cordially.

He did not remember me one little bit.

He nodded his head, gave my hand a perfunctory pump, and hurried on.

Ouch.

I wanted to be special and important. I wanted to be "in." But even more, I wanted my friends to see just how "in" I was.

So I think I understand a tiny fraction of Haman's OPC in this verse, at least a little. He scored the ultimate prize of "insider-ness"— a private time, sipping wine, with his new best friend, the King of the Known World. Laughing over an inside joke. Sniffing the perfumed air of the palace gardens. Looking out on the riff-raff below. Then, running home to regale his wife and friends with tales of his breathtaking gloriousness.

Meanwhile, the whole nation has its stomach in a collective knot. The city was "confused" says verse 15. Or literally, "tangled." Disturbed. Distressed. Perplexed.

This was Haman's goal all along: to gain personal significance at the cost of other people and their lives.

This is Evil's goal too. Let me state this big lesson this way: *The goal of evil is to gain personal pleasure or significance at the cost of other people and their lives, while justifying the price they pay in your own eyes.*

Evil may be a monster, but all to often she manifests as a beautiful monster. Alluring. Seductive. She does her fiendish deeds in the name of some exalted good, but, in the end, her true goal remains satisfying her own neediness.

Just maybe God can turn the tables on evil OPC. Let's find out.

Reflections

Reflections 1: We can only face evil OPC in other people to the extent that we have first faced it in our own heart.

Sometimes, we pay a lot of attention to the Hamans around us just to distract us from the Haman within us. So the Bible warns:

> You may be saying, "What terrible people you have been talking about!" But you are just as bad, and you have no excuse! When you say they are wicked and should be punished, you are condemning yourself, for you do these very same things. (Romans 2:1)

Haman spewed forth evil OPC, but he didn't necessarily realize it. He projected his own evil onto Mordecai. Or onto all the Jews. He projected it onto anybody but himself. Sometimes, we're not much different.

It's disconcerting that I can so easily overlook my own evil, and zero in on the evil in others. But we can only face evil in the world to the degree that we have faced it in our own hearts. We have to own up to our piece of the world's ugliness and our share of the world's pain. We are not only victims of OPC, we're also sources of it.

I won't dwell on this, because our focus is *other* people's craziness.

But where does that leave us? Are we all doomed to be a bunch of Hamans, and that's it?

Reflections 2: Christ Jesus, and him crucified, is God's only reconciling agent strong enough to unseat Haman from his throne.

Jesus dethroned evil. He did not do it by force or fiat. He did it by dying. His whole life was a qualification for his sacrificial death, and it was his death, not his life, that delivers us from evil. "Without the shedding of blood, there is no forgiveness of sins" (Hebrews 9:22).

How did it work?

Jesus first absorbed human evil, and then absorbed God's punishment for human evil. He absorbed our guilt and shame. He willingly took our place before the Supreme Court of Heaven, and acted as our stand-in, as if HE had perpetrated our sins. He was judged guilty of sins against God and mankind, and condemned to death. The execution was swift and complete. It was once for all. It was finished. The Cross of Christ effected our cleansing from sin, and our reconciliation with God—and did so without our help, advice, or assistance.

Pure grace.

There is no other solution. Jesus is God's only solution, God's only reconciling agent, strong enough to unseat Haman from his place of power in our lives.

Don't miss the logical progression of Scripture's logic in the book of Colossians:

Step one: we start out as evil-hearted Hamans, warring against God.

> This includes you who were once so far away from God. You were his enemies, separated from him by your evil thoughts and actions. (Colossians 1:21)

This fallen status is universal. It applies to all of us, no matter how religious, sweet, nice, generous, or church-going we may be. We may be very good people, but at the same time we have very bad parts lurking within.

Step two: Jesus paid the price to bring us back to God.

> [Y]et now he has brought you back as his friends. He has done this through his death on the cross in his own human body. As a result, he has brought you into the very presence of God, and you are holy and blameless as you stand before him without a single fault. (Colossians 1:22)

He alone is the agent of reconciliation. And he didn't miss even the tiniest speck of sin—thus enabling us to stand before God faultless. Even though we may fail a thousand times a day, his death was all-sufficient payment for those sins. Even the sins you're planning for later today. Past, present, or future—it doesn't matter. Christ shed his blood for them all.

But then does that mean that all are saved? that all are reconciled to God?

Step three: Reconciliation with God is offered to all but is received only by those who believe.

> But you must continue to believe this truth and stand in it firmly. Don't drift away from the assurance you received when you heard the Good News... (Colossians 1:23)

Personal trust in Jesus as your only hope, turning to him in faith and belief—that alone activates his reconciling power in your life. The moment you first believe, God immediately topples Haman's throne, delivers you from an evil heart, and implants a new heart within you.

Have you ever received Jesus? Have you embraced his monumental gift—when he died as your substitute, your sacrifice? Have you ever received Jesus? You can do that right now. You can receive him this very moment. When he died on the cross, he prayed, "Father, forgive them. For they do not know what they're doing."

God knows how clueless we all are. Even about our own evil.

And today, he is ready to forgive you. And over and over and over again, he will renew his forgiveness every morning till he calls you home.

Through a simple prayer, you can tell God that you are believing on Jesus as your only hope. That you are trusting him and his shed blood to forgive you for all the evil OPC that you've spewed into the world. You can ask Jesus to reconcile you to God. And he will. He promised to. Because no one has sinned more than Jesus can forgive.

Not even Haman. You just have to ask for his forgiveness; he won't cram it down your throat. Now it's time to see if Haman asked for it, because in God's universe, evildoers ultimately get what they ask for.

FOR REFLECTION AND DISCUSSION: Read Ephesians 2:1-10 and reflect on how God moves you from being his enemy to being his friend. What is our initial status with him? What does it become? What is the means by which our status is changed? And how do we lay hold of that means?

Describe a hypothetical relationship in which neither you nor your partner ever admitted your bad stuff? One in which you always blamed each other or someone else? What happens when you can't or won't own up to the evil OPC within? Discuss or journal your answers.

CHAPTER 6

Embrace Uncertainty

THE PHONE RANG, AND I ANSWERED it. A man I had never met told me, "Bill, our board met and unanimously decided to extend an offer to you to be the next senior pastor of our church." We had been praying and talking for a long time. Here it was, an invitation.

After I hung up, I had deep talks with Margi. We had a very demanding toddler running our lives, plus a baby on the way. We had both grown up in Chicago, and attended Chicago public schools our whole lives. All of our friends were in Chicago. Our families were in Chicago. All our familiar places were in Chicago. We knew the twists and turns of every street and alley, the best places for pizza, and the quickest way to Wrigley Field.

We had a job and a ministry we loved. Our church loved us and wanted us to stay.

We had just built our dream house and lived in it for only one year. I could walk to the pond out back and catch two- and three-pound bass before I left for work in the morning.

We were comfortable. We were secure. We were safe.

So why was God nagging at both of our hearts to leave all that behind, and go to—of all places—California? Even after we had prayed, "Lord, anywhere but California."

Mario Andretti, one of the greatest race car drivers of all time, said, "If things seem under control, you're just not going fast enough."

When Margi and I packed up and said good-bye to a lifetime of relationships and experiences in Chicago, we told each other, "Every once in a while, you've got to mix things up."

We also said, "Good Lord! What have we done now?" But that's for another chapter.

Jesus said, "I have come that you might have life, and that you might have it more abundantly" (John 10:10). The word "abundantly" comes from the Latin word that means "waves on the seashore." It connotes an overflowing, full, rich, large, sometimes out-of-control, life.

Jesus came so that you can have an overflowing, interesting, full, rich, large life. Not a half-hearted, safe, boring, predictable life. But a life that's like the ocean: powerful. Risky. Untamed.

Unfortunately, within every heart lurks a force that resists that life. In today's story, our hero, Queen Esther, has to face that force. What is it?

Risk-aversion.

The world's OPC-perpetrators have produced such a scary world that it's a natural desire to bubble wrap everything in sight. In an attempt to shield ourselves from OPC, we inadvertently slip into a safe, bland, boring, vanilla life. By seeking to save our life, we lose it. We settle for a half-life and call it Christianity. We have become the exact opposites of the man who overturned the moneychangers in the temple.

Sometimes, combating OPC summons us to the path of most resistance. Here are the steps Esther took as she walked into the furnace of danger.

Admit the Danger

When Mordecai learned what had been done, he tore his clothes, put on sackcloth and ashes, and went out into the city, crying with a loud and bitter wail . He stood outside the gate of the palace, for no one was allowed to enter while wearing clothes of mourning. And as news of the king's decree reached all the provinces, there was great mourning among the Jews. They fasted, wept, and wailed, and many people lay in sackcloth and ashes. When Queen Esther's maids and eunuchs came and told her about Mordecai, she was deeply distressed. She sent clothing to him to replace the sackcloth, but he refused it. Then Esther sent for Hathach, one of the king's eunuchs who had been appointed as her attendant. She ordered him to go to Mordecai and find out what was troubling him and why he was in mourning. (Esther 4:1-5)

When Margi and I first moved from Chicago to California, we were blissfully unaware of a few things. Underline blissfully.

Neither one of us had ever seen a black widow spider until one built a big, messy web by the front door of our new house, perfectly poised to reach our inquisitive two-year old daughter. Our friend squashed it like it was no big deal, while a serene smile masked my internal freaking out.

Neither one of us had ever lived near rattlesnakes, until our neighbor warned us that he found a baby rattlesnake in his garage.

Don't even get me started about the scorpion that stung me in the heel in my own bedroom. We thought, *Lord, we're living inside an Egyptian curse.* Life in rustic northern

California carries risks that life in urban Chicago doesn't, and we were unaware.

On some things, my wife and I are slow learners. But one lesson that's starting to sink in is this: no matter where you go, no matter what your position, every *real* life has its dangers. You can't hide from danger, from risk, from struggle, and from problems and have a real life at the same time.

When they heard of Haman's planned holocaust, all the Jews of Persia went into mourning. All except one. One Jew hadn't heard the news, because she was sheltered in her palace.

Queen Esther was blissfully unaware of the mortal threat to her people. I picture her dressed in the finest silks, plucking grapes from overflowing fruit bowls, sharing laughter with her ladies in waiting, and wondering what all that caterwauling outside was about. Comfortable. Pampered. Creating familiar routines. Alienated from the real life of the streets.

The upheaval that dragged her into the palace in the first place, has imperceptibly morphed into an even greater danger: complacency.

You can have a safe life. You can have a comfortable life. You can have a pampered life.

But you can't hide from danger and have the abundant life Jesus promised. God knows that the trauma of rising above OPC activates a capacity for life that would not otherwise be activated.

I'm not suggesting you seek out high-risk activities, like bungee jumping, skydiving, or listening to disco. You don't need to create your own danger; it will seek you out. And when it does, you can run, but you can't hide. And the more you try to hide, the more you'll discover that the walls that shelter you eventually squeeze the life out of you. To be alive requires that you stand in the batter's box, open-eyed, ready to swing at every pitch OPC hurls your direction. It's time for Esther to get off the bench.

Understand your Privileges

So Hathach went out to Mordecai in the square in front of the palace gate. Mordecai told him the whole story and told him how much money Haman had promised to pay into the royal treasury for the destruction of the Jews. Mordecai gave Hathach a copy of the decree issued in Susa that called for the death of all Jews, and he asked Hathach to show it to Esther. He also asked Hathach to explain it to her and to urge her to go to the king to beg for mercy and plead for her people. So Hathach returned to Esther with Mordecai's message. (Esther 4:6-9)

Here's a head's up: as you read these upcoming chapters, notice that Esther and Mordecai never talk face to face in this chapter. They communicate through servants who bounce back and forth between them, like a ping-pong ball. I count four full round trips—eight lengths, four laps. More about that later.

So finally, Esther gets brought into the nasty loop of doom. She hears Haman's plot. It had to feel like a punch in the stomach, especially since she knew Haman. And now, the evil Mastermind has wormed his way into a special friendship with the king.

Esther must have been shaking in her Ferragamos.

So what does Mordecai tell her to do? Let's view Mordecai as a kind of ancient life-coach for Esther—and for all of us, if we'll listen.

So how does he coach this young woman, who is trapped in a palace and a marriage that she doesn't want, who has just found out that her husband's BFF is a latent mass murderer, and that she happens to be on his hit list? What does he say to a young woman who's had her worst ever "terrible, horrible, no good, very bad day?"

He "commands" her to go in before the king and "beg for mercy," and "plead" for her people.

Mordecai urges Esther, the Queen, to go and pursue compassionate grace from the king. Don't sit back and hope that it comes to you, Esther. Get up, and go get it. Pursue it. Seek it. Ask for it. Take the initiative.

The U.S. Gold depository at Fort Knox houses the nation's gold supply, about 4,750 tons. The vault is protected by a blast-proof door that weighs 24 tons. No one official has the combination to the vault. Different officials are given different combinations known only to them, and each one has to dial a different combination on a different dial to open the vault.

By today's prices, that gold is worth about $275 billion.

Wouldn't you like to have the combinations to that vault?

What if I told you that, if you have Jesus, you have a better treasure than Fort Knox? Because when you received Jesus, God opened up the treasures of heaven to you. Jesus dialed the combination, and threw open the vault. It's packed with riches and treasures you can't begin to count. You'll find power in times of weakness, healing in times of illness, hope, in times of despair, help in time of need, and abundant resources for every trial. You'll find love, courage, wisdom, kindness, protection, care, provision, and blessings. You'll find Jesus, and "in him lie hidden all the treasures of wisdom and knowledge" (Colossians 2:3, NKJV).

Why did God open his treasury to you? Was it because you were a decent, OPC-free human being? No. Because you deserved it? No. He did it because Jesus died as your substitute and rose again, and you humbly received him. So now, all the treasures of divine grace that belong to Jesus also belong to you.

So, what are you waiting for? Go get it! When Mordecai coaches Esther to seek the king's mercy, he operates from the premise of a verse that wouldn't be written for several centuries:

> So let us come boldly to the throne of our gracious God. There we will receive his mercy, and we will find grace to help us when we need it. (Hebrews 4:16)

There is nothing you need that isn't sitting in heaven right now in God's wide-open vault. There was nothing Esther needed that wasn't equally available to her, too. When OPC fires its worst at you, God stands ready to deliver his best.

This is an all-important truth for Christ's followers to understand. The answer to Other People's Craziness begins with Other People's Kindness—and in every case, the Prime Mover of Other People's Kindness is God.

God's matchless grace is the hope of the world.

Lance B. Latham—a pastor and the founder of a world-wide kids' ministry called Awana—counseled me as a youth pastor to "teach the kids their riches in Christ." He might have been thinking of St. Paul's statement:

> Just think! Though I did nothing to deserve it, and though I am the least deserving Christian there is, I was chosen for this special joy of telling the Gentiles about the endless treasures available to them in Christ. (Ephesians 3:8)

What "endless treasures"?

1.) The endless treasure of a new identity. When you received Christ he peeled off the accumulated labels of a lifetime, and re-labeled you according to your new identity in union with Christ. You are beloved, powerful, capable, forgiven, adopted, and declared righteous. You have access to

God. You have authority. If you have Christ, you have the treasure of a new identity. God labels you just as he labels Christ.

2.) You also have the endless treasure of perfect provision. When God looked down the corridors of time and previewed your life, he saw everything you would ever need, and made sure it would be there for you just in time. He is called, "Yahweh Yireh," "The Lord Who Will Provide" (Genesis 22:14). God has provided everything you need for your present happiness. In his wisdom, he has provided everything possible to achieve the best possible long-term outcomes in your life, even though you might not feel like it.

3.) Don't forget the endless treasure of new powers. You have *the power of prayer.* You can approach God any time, anywhere, in any situation or mood. The throne of grace beckons you. You have *the power of the Holy Spirit.* He dwells inside you, and is working 24/7 to transform you into your deepest, truest, most glorious self. His power is only as far away as your next moment of faith. You have *the power of the Word of God* (Hebrews 4:12). As you build God's Word into your heart, you create an impregnable fortress of confidence and joy. You have *the power of dominion* (Genesis 1:26,28 and Romans 5:17). God has given you the right to rule and reign in your own life, under his mighty Lordship.

The endless treasures of grace are just waiting for you.

The better you understand your privileges, the more you discover you do not need to slink through life as a victim. Especially when OPC turns threatening.

This is the discovery Esther is right in the middle of.

And this is exactly where risk-aversion rears its cowardly head.

Identify Inner Resistance

> Then Esther told Hathach to go back and relay this message to Mordecai: "The whole world knows that anyone who appears before the king in his inner court without being invited is doomed to die unless the king holds out his gold scepter. And the king has not called for me to come to him in more than a month." So Hathach gave Esther's message to Mordecai. (Esther 4:10-12)

This is a story about life and death. You might not be facing a death sentence, but every one of us faces a half-death sentence every day.

Let me remind you of how Esther got into the palace, and then ask a question.

Esther became queen in spite of herself. The King banished his previous Queen, and then felt sorry for himself. So, he held an international beauty and sex contest. All young women were entered, even against their will. Congratulations, Esther, you win.

Now, she lives in the palace as the Queen of the Persian Empire. The chief wife of King Xerxes. A title she never asked for, and a marriage she didn't want. Plus, she's not his only wife. And she's not his only lover. He probably still sleeps with a different woman every night.

So answer this question: Even though Esther has the title of Queen, and even though she lives in the palace, and even though she's married to the most powerful man in the known world, *is she really living?*

As a little boy, I loved monster movies. Not slasher movies, but old, black and white monster movies. Frankenstein. Wolfman. The Mummy. Of all the scary monsters, the creepiest monsters to me were zombies. The undead. Tormented souls trapped in a middle place that wasn't life but wasn't death either. Eyes half-open. Vacant stares. Pliable wills.

Most people are only half-alive because most people choose the path of least resistance most of the time.

And if that's all you ever choose, here's the kind of life you'll have: the path of least resistance is the path of least excitement, and the path of least fruitfulness.

Here reclines Esther, luxuriating on the path of least resistance. She's beginning to get comfortable in the crazy, ridiculous, dangerous world of the palace. She has grown so comfortable, that when she is asked to save her whole nation from destruction, what does she think about?

Self-preservation.

And the crazy thing is that the kind of life she has now isn't worth preserving. It's a half-life. She's a Queen without power. A wife without a real marriage. A beauty without appreciation. A Jew without a people.

Is that why she was born? Is that it? That safe, boring, predictable half-life that Esther's settling into?

So she fears the king's policy: anybody who comes before him uninvited is automatically put to death. The only exception would be if the king held out his golden scepter. And judging by the past month, he's not interested in seeing her.

That means she has a choice between risking her neck to gain the life she really wants, or playing it safe to keep the zombie-life she's come to know.

But make no mistake: to keep the life she's come to know means caving in to other people's craziness—accepting it, coalescing with it, and becoming one with it. And, worst of all, it means redefining her OPC-dominated life as normal, healthy, and good.

For Esther to stay in the palace and let her people die, she will have to sell-out to OPC.

You and I face a mini-version of that same temptation every day. Each of us has a voice inside whispering, "Just go along to get along. Don't make waves. Yeah, it's bad, but it's the way it is. It's evil, but you can't fight it."

If that's the only voice you ever follow, you are going to live a very long, very safe, very dull life. And the rest of us will have to deal with your craziness. Recognize this inner resistance for what it is: making a god out of safety.

Embrace Uncertainty

Mordecai sent back this reply to Esther: "Don't think for a moment that you will escape there in the palace when all other Jews are killed. If you keep quiet at a time like this, deliverance for the Jews will arise from some other place, but you and your relatives will die. What's more, who can say but that you have been elevated to the palace for just such a time as this?" (Esther 4:13,14)

In 1910, U.S. President Theodore Roosevelt gave a speech in Paris. It has become one of the most quoted and most inspiring speeches of all time:

It is not the critic who counts: not the man who points out how the strong man stumbles or where the doer of deeds could have done better. The credit belongs to the man who is actually in the arena, whose face is marred by dust and sweat and blood, who strives valiantly, who errs and comes up short again and again, because there is no effort without error or shortcoming, but who knows the great enthusiasms, the great devotions, who spends himself for a worthy cause; who, at the best, knows, in the end, the triumph of high achievement, and who, at the worst, if he fails, at least he fails while daring greatly, so that his place shall never be with those cold and timid souls who knew neither victory nor defeat.

Mordecai puts his finger on a drive that exists in every human heart: the drive to create a hassle-free life. We enter life with a deeply rooted desire for equilibrium.

He sees this in Esther. Notice how he addresses it.

"Do not think in your heart," he says (literally). Apparently, Esther suffers from Disordered Internal Dialog. One part of her heart is telling another part of her heart to play it safe.

In this Scripture, Mordecai forever confronts the voices that will turn us into Christianized zombies. Because he's learned the secret: the palace offers safety from harm, but not from lifelessness. Ditto for a mansion. Or a lot of money. Or a new trophy wife. Or a wealthy spouse. Or dating a cheerleader. Real life always has uncertainty.

Resist uncertainty, resist life.

Embrace uncertainty, embrace life.

Mordecai delivers one of the Bible's most quotable punchlines: *Who knows whether Esther has been elevated to the palace for such a time as this?*

"For such a time as this..."

There is a window that opens and shuts on each opportunity. Time is scarce. It is not an unlimited commodity, at least not in this lifetime. The clock is ticking.

You get one chance to seize life; don't waste it. Don't numb yourself to the life of your dreams.

You might worry, "It's too late. I've already numbed myself. I have wasted my life." Okay—then don't waste what's left of it. Besides, the Bible offers a most amazing promise. God is the Lord of Time, and he promises to restore to you the years that you have wasted, if you'll only let him (Joel 2:25). A doctor might restore your health. A counselor might restore your hope. An advisor might restore your money. But only

91

God can restore your years. No matter how much of life you've wasted, grace means it's never too late for a "do-over."

In this place, at this time, for such a time as this, do whatever you can to seize life for yourself, and to support others in that same quest.

Esther faces a choice that every person bombarded with OPC must face: she can hunker down in her half-alive status quo, or she can risk the life she has to gain the life she wants. Esther will either rise to her full stature as royalty, or go down in history with a long list of nobodies who didn't answer the summons to greatness. You will either acquiesce to OPC, or exercise the risk-taking faith that moves into the danger zone and leaves the outcome to God.

You have to risk the life you have to gain the life you want.

𐎹 𐎼 𐎸 𐎣 𐎹 𐎻

Reflections

Reflections 1: The onlooking world waits for you to lay hold of the real life that Christ has for you.

Esther and Mordecai never talk face to face in this chapter. Instead, servants shuttle messages back and forth between them.

The information they carry is sensitive. Nobody in the palace knows that Esther is a Jew—except, perhaps, these servants, assuming they carry oral, not written messages. This is the Author's first hint that there may be sympathetic allies for the Jews; friends who might stand up for their cause, and even more importantly, be open to their message of faith.

Let these servants picture your unsaved friends and family. They're watching you. In a sense, their future depends on you. If Jesus Christ doesn't make a difference against OPC in your life, then there's no hope anywhere.

Whether it's your neighborhood, your school, your family, your workplace, your subdivision, your dorm, or your apartment, the onlooking world waits for you to lay hold your real life in Christ before they will believe a word you tell them about Jesus.

They want to see if all you have is another version of the same old craziness they've lived with all their lives, or if you have something truly different. If you can't offer a way out of the craziness, who will?

Reflections 2: Nobody can intimidate you but you.

The one thing Esther fears most is that golden scepter. Either the king will extend it toward her, and let her live. Or he'll withhold it, and let her die. Teddy Roosevelt mentioned "those cold and timid souls who knew neither victory nor defeat."

Right now, Esther is one of those cold and timid souls.

Whose fault is that? The king's? Haman's? Mordecai's? The Devil's?

You might disagree with me, but that's okay. I'll just ask you to think about this: the only person that can intimidate you is you. You do it to yourself.

To be intimidated means to say, *I make myself timid in your presence.*

Whether the OPC perpetrator is scary, dangerous, mean, big, powerful, or nasty. Whether he or she is richer, stronger, smarter, more spiritual, or more beautiful. And whether you feel scared, or threatened, or in danger. None of it ultimately matters.

What matters is whether or not you, as a child of God, make yourself timid in another person's presence. The Bible affirms, "For God has not given us a spirit of fear and timidity, but of power, love, and self-discipline" (2 Timothy 1:7). If you really want to deal with OPC, then no matter how you feel, you have to manifest a different spirit. How? By a muscular faith.

That golden scepter, that thing that scares you that looks like death, that thing that you've been avoiding, that thing that makes you feel powerless—that very thing holds the key to real life for you and those around you. Remember: "If things seem under control, you're just not going fast enough."

Jesus taught: "If you try to keep your life for yourself, you will lose it. But if you give up your life for me, you will find true life" (Luke 9:24).

And he practiced what he preached. Jesus headed straight for Calvary, where he lost the life he had, and gained the life he really wanted—the life he was destined for. No risk, no reward. No guts, no glory. No Cross, no crown.

FOR REFLECTION AND DISCUSSION: What do you think about the statement that nobody can intimidate you but you. Agree or disagree? Why? Review the steps in the method of evil. How does evil spin its web? How might you not realize it till it's too late? What evils tend to wear you down? How does God, by his grace, enable you to rise above?

CHAPTER 7

Forget the Rules

MY ATTORNEY, WHO IS ALSO my wife, told me I had to start this chapter with a disclaimer: *Only an unthinking buffoon would do what I am about to describe, and you should never, under any circumstances, do something as reckless, foolhardy, and illegal as the following. The writer did this deed as a youthful indiscretion, and now repents of it and urges you to never imitate it or anything like it.*

"I wonder how fast this rental car can go," I mused. I was driving across a barren stretch of Colorado, heading toward a seminar. A ribbon of road shimmered straight and flat through the sunlit chaparral. Mine was the only car in sight. I had always said that God created me for luxury, not speed, but this opportunity was hard to resist.

Immediately, my ultra-obedient inner child piped in, "It's wrong to speed." I had grown up in a fundamentalist church. Rule-keeping was screwed tightly into the socket of my psyche. My life defined the phrase, "straight and narrow." I held the distinction of being one of a minute handful of gung-ho students who actually attended high school on "National

Cut Day." While virtually all my fellow students played hooky, I sat dutifully (and self-righteously, I must confess) in my hard wooden seat. "Rules are rules," I told myself.

I told myself that again as I contemplated how fast my rented sedan could go. I sighed, "Rules are rules." Suddenly another voice—a voice that magically pumped adrenaline into my system—answered, "Rules are made to be broken."

In that memorable moment, something clicked inside me. I warned my ultra-obedient inner child to pipe down and buckle up. I felt a sly smile creep across my face. I felt my fingers grip the wheel. I felt my foot hit the accelerator. I leaned forward like Snoopy chasing the Red Baron. I felt the G-force push me into the seat.

"Just how fast *can* this thing go?"

> Then Esther sent this reply to Mordecai: "Go and gather together all the Jews of Susa and fast for me. Do not eat or drink for three days, night or day. My maids and I will do the same. And then, though it is against the law, I will go in to see the king. If I must die, I am willing to die." So Mordecai went away and did as Esther told him. (Esther 4:15-17)

God created us for life. To God, *life* means more than simply the opposite of death. The Hebrew word for life conveys the idea of really living. It envisions life with energy, motivation, emotion, thought, purpose, and satisfaction. That's the life that Jesus lived. And that's the life he wants to recreate in us.

So God sets life before us. Yet two enemies subvert all our attempts to seize it, one internal, one external. The internal enemy, risk aversion, clamors for the path of least resistance. The external enemy, OPC, badgers you to sit in your corner like a compliant school child with hands folded and lips zipped.

Esther faces a terrible dilemma: in order to seize life for her people and herself, she must approach the king. But there are *rules* about this. The king has not summoned her, and rules are rules, right? Not to mention that the price of a "pop-in" is quite capital. After all, we have to be reasonable about these things.

Or do we? What constitutes a "reasonable" response to holocaust? To approach the king is to invite death. To not approach the king is to invite death too, on a scale too horrible to imagine. Which will Esther choose?

In one glorious moment, Esther shoves her risk-aversion aside and crashes through the towering walls of OPC. She will walk into the jaws of death to seize life for herself and her people.

The Author retells Esther's words in four phrases. If you ever hope to rise above OPC, you'll organize your soul around each of these powerful phrases.

Gather Allies

Then Esther sent this reply to Mordecai: "Go and gather together all the Jews of Susa..."

A pastor described the summer he spent digging a trench for a large pipeline.[2] He was given a shovel and a place to dig. His boss told him to dig a trench six feet deep and three feet wide.

The work was brutal, but by noon he had dug a hole so deep he couldn't see out anymore. He was tired, sore, sweaty, dirty, and discouraged. Plus, he was alone in this blasted hole he couldn't see out of.

The more he thought about how much trench had to be dug, the more depressed he got. The work seemed impossible. He felt like giving up.

Suddenly, he broke through to the ditch-digger in the next hole. The pastor described how all the workers watched in amazed relief as, one by one, the dirt walls came down. Now, instead of being alone in a hole, the men were joined together in a trench.

What felt like an impossibly overwhelming task suddenly felt possible. But not until the workers were all connected.

When Esther decided to approach the king, she gathered her people first. "All" her people. She didn't skip anyone.

Because real life is not a solo occupation. From the beginning God decreed, "It is not good for people to be alone." Not even God is alone. Long before the planets and stars and worlds and angels, there was God. But God was not alone, because he exists in an eternal community we call the Trinity. One undivided God eternally existing in three intimate, unconfounded Persons.

No religion has anything like it: the Creator himself is singular, but not alone.

And when God made us in his own image, he wired us with a drive to forge connections with others. He created us to stand shoulder-to-shoulder and face-to-face. He saw the OPC coming and knew we needed friends. Allies.

Before you stick out your neck, make sure somebody's got your back. And the first and most important somebody in your life is your spouse—assuming you're married. If you are married, you are no longer two, but one. And if you're going to stick your neck out—if you're going nose to nose with a golden scepter that will either make you or break you—both you and your spouse had better be on the exact same page.

Or else you'll damage your bond. And you'll add fuel to any marital OPC already coming your way. And you'll be firing off your own OPC in your spouse's direction. In marriage, as in business or parenting or any close relationship, the decision to move toward danger has to be mutual. Neither party gets to unilaterally say, "Honey, I'm cashing in the nest egg so I can become a rock star!"

If you're single (for whatever reason), it's equally important to have allies in your life. I became a pastor as a single guy, and stayed that way for several years, despite the best efforts of a whole lot of sweet, little old ladies who kept trying to marry me off. I understand the pressures and joys of single life. I jumped into small groups and ministries, and found my "spiritual family." I encourage you to plug in to healthy groups at church or other places. Somebody has to have your back.

Whether it's the alliance called your marriage, your church, your buddies on the team, your colleagues at work, the ladies in the subdivision, or your squad in the barracks, it's best to connect with somebody else to experience God's abundant life.

Before Esther risked her neck, she made sure somebody had her back.

Prepare Your Spirit

"...[A]nd fast for me. Do not eat or drink for three days, night or day. My maids and I will do the same..."

Don't expect the fullest possible victory over OPC if you neglect your spirit.

Esther calls for a period of fasting. Fasting means going without food or drink for a set time, while engaging in periods of intensified prayer.

First, let's notice that this is the closest this book comes to mentioning God so far. Here we are through four chapters. Esther's life is a roller coaster. She has been oppressed, manipulated, degraded, victimized, and God hasn't even been mentioned yet.

Some scholars find this troubling. Almost two centuries ago, Adam Clarke commented, "What a strange thing, that still we hear nothing of prayer, nor of God! What is the ground on which we can account for this total silence? I know it not."3

May I respectfully suggest that, in Esther, God's silence is by design? The storyteller makes her point by omission. She is telling us it's okay if most of the time our lives feel as if God is hidden. It's okay if God seems silent or absent. We can be doing everything right and still feel as if God is playing hide and seek. I've felt like that. I suspect you have too. And Esther felt like that.

Yet she fasts and prays and wants her people to do the same.

Why? Maybe it's because she knows the great mystery: *You cannot experience your abundant life through natural means alone.* An abundant life requires a supernatural core. The craziness in your life is a gnarly branch of a depraved and fallen world. Only Jesus can uproot it from your life. The abundant life is supernatural; there is more to it than meets the eye.

Many people look to purely natural factors for life: money, education, power, position, muscles, good looks, prestige, personality, image, size of your house, size of your pants, nice car, high I.Q., sexual skills, who you know.

And all these factors do matter, and they do affect your life. But even if you had all of them to the max, you still might not feel really alive.

Real life transcends the natural order. Real life touches the supernatural. It is sacred.

Sensing this, some people layer a transcendent value over their otherwise natural approach to life. They'll add in meditation, "giving back," karma, luck, fate, the x-factor, or some other nebulous force. Anything to scratch the transcendent itch we all carry by virtue of creation in God's image.

The problem with all these solutions is simple: they are impersonal. They possess no soul. No personhood. No identity other than a mindless force supposedly standing one or two rungs above nature on the ladder of existence.

This puts the typical person in the awkward position of possessing more life than the force they're counting on for life.

The true supernatural, transcendent, sacred vector of every human life can only be found in the Person of our Lord Jesus Christ—the ultimate Person, the untarnished Human, the One who lived the fullest life possible and invited us to follow his path.

Real life comes from Jesus living in you and living through you. It comes from faith. It comes from the Holy Spirit, from the Word of God, and from grace.

If you subtract the supernatural person of Christ, you may be rich, beautiful, and successful, but you won't possess real life. It's only when Jesus fills your spirit with his presence and grace that your life can be full.

Esther's mission: to stand before the king so she could save the lives of her people.

Esther's hope: that he would extend his golden scepter, giving her access to the throne room.

So she commanded her people to fast and pray. So what?

Esther's approach: Long before she plunked her diamond-encrusted foot into Xerxes' throne room, Esther set foot in a better, stronger, higher throne room first. She entered the throne room of heaven. She trusted that no matter what happened on earth, the King of kings would extend his golden scepter.

Plus, she reminded all the Jews in the capital city exactly where their help would come from.

If you feel used up, alone, depressed, or if you feel frustrated or bored, or if you feel as if every road is a dead end, then ask yourself, "Am I taking care of my spirit? Am I relying too much on the natural realm and too little on the supernatural promises of God? Do I touch the invisible universe through Jesus? Do I live a spiritual life?"

Life in the Spirit awakens parts of your heart you never knew existed.

Esther prepared her spirit. That made her ready for the next leap of faith.

Forget the Rules

"And then, though it is against the law, I will go in to see the king..."

Here's the picture I get of Esther: she's a woman who has always stayed between the lines. She does what is expected. She does what she's supposed to do. Except for now. For one shining moment, she swerves outside the lines. And guess what she finds out there: a real life. Outside the lines. Outside the box. Breaking through the arbitrary rules imposed by herself and the crazies in her world.

Something inside of her clicked and Esther crashed through a lifetime of rules. At first her rules protected her. But the closer Esther came to real life, the more the rules only restricted her. So finally, she said, "Enough! Even though it is against the law, I'll do it."

Now, don't get crazy on me. This doesn't mean you can break the speed limit—unless you're in parts of Montana or on the Autobahn, where I'm told there are no limits. Or unless, of course, you find yourself on some sort of a personal quest in Colorado's wasteland. This doesn't mean you can tell your boss you're going to do things your own way from now on. Nor does it mean you can disobey the Bible. Nor can you break the rules of law and order that keep our society safe for all. That's not what I'm talking about.

I'm talking about the cautious, self-restrictive, self-protective rules that *you* put on your life, or that other people have tried to put on your life, or that you insist on putting on other people's lives. Those rules.

Forget those rules.

Hit the gas.

You will not find real life by setting yourself in an emotional playpen of rules and regulations and steps and seminars and recipes and procedures.

You will find life by setting yourself right smack in front of important things that scare you and make you feel little, and then plunging ahead not knowing the outcome, because you trust the One who holds the outcome in the palm of his hand.

A young man named David was ridiculed by his big brothers. *You're too little. You're just a kid. This is a big man's*

103

world. Go home to Daddy. All of life pressured David to live by somebody else's rules. But David jettisoned the rules, slaughtered a giant, and freed his people from their enemies.

Daniel shook free of the rules when he prayed three times a day, even though the king commanded him not to.

Peter ignored the rules when he proclaimed—against the law—Jesus as Lord. He told the Religious Council on Crushing Spirits and Controlling Lives, properly called the Sanhedrin, "we must obey God rather than human authority" (Acts 5:29).

Even Jesus said *forget the rules.* He went into the temple and overturned tables. He attacked the hypocritical worshippers there with a home-made whip. He shocked the religious establishment by eating with ritually unwashed hands. He scandalized the respectable crowd by mingling his life with hookers and cheats.

Jesus was wild at heart. Untamable.

Your spirit soars high above the world's rules.

OPC is dedicated to crushing your spirit. It insists you keep a low profile. If you are going to stand out, or be great, or be special, or be alive, OPC will oppose you. Don't be so surprised. The crazies will strain every fiber of their being to rein you in, hold you down, and kick you out. OPC often arrives special delivery via other people's rules. They will tell you to be sensible, be cautious, remember your reputation, don't make waves, be proper, steer a middle course, and all but hitch your pants up to your armpits. Never get that tattoo, or piercing. And never dye your hair that crazy color.

God loves bland, right?

No.

Last time I read anything about Jesus, he was all color and spice.

As followers of Jesus, we are guided by the Holy Spirit as he applies God's Word, studied and internalized, to our conscience. Anybody else's rules are just another variety of Other People's Craziness.

I'm suggesting that you take all of the rules that were whispered in your ear growing up, and all of the rules that were drummed into you in church, and all of the rules that you created for yourself because they make you feel safe and allow you to congratulate yourself while condemning the guy on the other end of the caution-scale—and run all your rules through the shredder.

And if that gets you into trouble, at least you won't be bored.

Get Real

"If I must die, I am willing to die."

I always feel a little sick when somebody says, "I just *know* that God is going to ____. [Fill in the blank: heal me, get me this job, win the lotto for me, bring me the man/woman of my dream, make me rich, take away the urge to drink, etc.].

Confidence is good. Faith is good.

A reality check is good, too. Esther does a reality check. I'll go before the king and if I perish, I perish.

Maybe you have been told that faith means being certain, and if you sound uncertain you don't have faith. And if you don't have faith, your prayers won't come true.

Christian clichés have a way of sucking joy out of life.

We are inundated with the "positive thinking," "laws of attraction" messages that good things will come to you if you can only manifest enough "positive energy." We hear this stuff even in the church.

It bears more resemblance to pagan *karma* than to the message and teaching of God's Word.

Plus, it didn't work very well for Jesus and his followers, many of whom suffered mightily. Many of whom were martyred.

And what does it mean when all that positivity doesn't work out for you? When your broken down old car barely limps along, and your nails are broken, and your kids need shoes, and money is too tight to do it all?

All the Christian clichés that make God a dispenser of happy pills wind up loading unhappy people with a heavy basket of guilt and shame.

Jesus came to set you free.

Faith does not mean being certain. Faith means acting in spite of being uncertain. Let this truth deep inside your heart: you can be doing everything right with God, and the outcomes on earth still seem like a mess.

Yes, sometimes, you might have a certain faith, like David when he confronted Goliath:

> "Today the LORD will conquer you, and I will kill you and cut off your head. And then I will give the dead bodies of your men to the birds and wild animals, and the whole world will know that there is a God in Israel!" (1 Samuel 17:46)

But other times, faith feels uncertain, like Shadrach, Meshach and Abednego, about to be thrown into a fiery furnace:

> "If that is the case, our God whom we serve is able to deliver us from the burning fiery furnace, and He will deliver us from your hand, O king. But if not, let it be known to you, O king, that we do not serve your gods, nor will we worship the gold image which you have set up." (Daniel 3:17, 18, NKJV)

"But if not..." There's the reality check. But if he doesn't deliver us... But if he doesn't heal us... But if he doesn't provide the money, the food, the relationship...

But if not, I will still embrace the risk and cast myself on God's grace anyway.

Esther has faith, but it is an uncertain faith. Uncertain faith is a wonderful faith. It's a valid faith. A great faith. A bigger faith. You don't have to psych yourself up into certainty before you exercise faith. In fact, it's the other way around. If all life's uncertainties were erased, you wouldn't need faith. And you wouldn't need God either.

I'll go to the king, and if I perish, I perish.

She doesn't sugar-coat the danger. She may very well die. What an incredible attitude! Esther doesn't dwell in la-la land. She stares danger in the face and doesn't flinch—at least not for long.

True faith means setting your heart in front of ultimate danger—sweaty palms, sick feeling in your gut, mind reeling, heart pounding, death or embarrassment or failure at your heels—and taking that step toward life which really feels like a step toward death.

In that moment—and not one second before—you discover what only the unintimidated discover: Christ is in you with supernatural power and strength. And even if you perish, you still gain the life you always wanted anyway. Welcome home, faithful Christian.

Esther is about to wade neck deep into OPC.

I guarantee you, she wasn't bored.

The path of least resistance is the path of least aliveness. So get out of your comfort zone. Choose life and watch your Unseen Father launch an operation you never saw coming. But that has to wait for two more chapters.

Oh. One last thing...
102 mph.

Reflections

Reflections 1: Life with God can be dangerous.

Daniel got thrown into a lion's den. Peter walked out of a boat, to walk on water, only to sink a few moments later. Three friends got tossed into a fiery furnace. Esther must appear unsummoned before the king, and odds are strong that she will have her head chopped off.

Life with God can be dangerous, because God does not make himself our heavenly bubble-wrap.

But we Christians don't like that side of the equation, so we all too often turn God into His Royal Harmlessness. We make him His Infinite Niceness. We look to him for warm fuzzies and golden sunsets on scenic calendars and Facebook posts. We want glory clouds and gold dust, when he's giving opportunities to build muscle and grit.

The Bible reveals that there are angels flying around the throne of God, calling out God's essential core quality: and they are not saying "Nice! Nice! Nice is the Lord of Nap Time."

They are saying "Holy! Holy! Holy! is the Lord of Armies" (Isaiah 6:3). Whatever else holiness is, it is something that makes people who see it fall over (John), tremble (Daniel), get sick to their stomachs (Daniel), and feel like they're going to explode (Isaiah). No, God isn't nice, comfortable, dull, or lethargic.

The great apologist of our grandparents' era, Dorothy Sayers, wrote,

> If this [Jesus] is dull, then what, in heaven's name, is worthy to be called exciting? The people who hanged Christ never, to do them justice, accused him of being a bore—on the contrary, they thought him too dynamic to be safe. It has been left for later generations to muffle up that shattering personality and surround him with an atmosphere of tedium. We have very efficiently pared the claws of the Lion of Judah, certified him 'meek and mild,' and recommend him as a fitting household pet for pale curates and pious old ladies. To those who knew him, however, he in no way suggests a milk-and-water person; they objected to him as a dangerous firebrand.

Which leads to...

Reflections 2: Jesus was wild at heart.

Jesus pushed people to places they didn't think they wanted to go. He made them draw conclusions they didn't realize they needed to think.

Was he being unkind?

Not at all.

He was unshackling prisoners from chains of self-deception, and self-limitation. He was making their redemption real.

And when you received Jesus as your Savior, he came to live in you and through you. The power he exerts moment-by-moment, day after day, reflects his untamed heart.

A tame life longs for a tame God. A mildly powerful life longs for a semi-potent God. But a free, unfettered life requires a sovereign, illimitable God.

Disneyworld offers two rides at opposite ends of the thrill spectrum. The oh-so gentle "Small World" takes visitors on a calm boat ride through a maze of animated dolls singing over and over the same tune in countless languages. I thought I would lose my mind by the fourth time my toddler-aged daughter dragged me on that ride. To this day, I suffer flashbacks at the merest hint of the "Small World" tune.

At the opposite end of the thrill spectrum, "Space Mountain" offers a roller coaster ride in virtual pitch-blackness. You can't see what twist or drop or turn or flip comes next, so all you can do is hang on and enjoy the ride.

Christ-in-you is pushing you toward "Space Mountain" but a self-protective corner of your risk-averse soul prefers spending the rest of your life on "It's a Small World."

Have you redefined God? Have you (in your imagination of him) clipped his wings and pared his claws? Don't answer, because the only way to really tell is by your life:

When was the last time you stuck your neck out in sheer faith—in stomach-wrenching faith—in Jesus?

Reflections 3: The severity of God is better than the niceness of mankind.

When I was in my twenties, I had surgery on my shoulder: it kept dislocating. A surgeon fixed it.

After surgery came physical therapy. That therapist made me bend my shoulder joint till I wanted to scream. Was he being nice? No. Was he being loving? Yes. The severity of a physical therapist is better than the niceness of anybody else who would pat my head say, "Poor little bunny; don't you move that silly old shoulder of yours." That oh-so-nice advice would have crippled me for life.

If God is pushing us to the deep end of faith's pool, so be it. I'd rather serve an untamed God and feel truly alive, than spend even one minute more listening to those animated dolls singing "It's a small, small world."

FOR DISCUSSION AND PERSONAL REFLECTION: How rule oriented are you? Does that help or hurt your life? Have you ever had physical therapy? How did it feel? How did you react emotionally? What was the goal? What might that teach you about God? How do you respond when God feels absent? What might you say to others who feel the same way?

CHAPTER 8

Flex Your Muscle

ILEEN WARNED ME, "Watch out for Larry. He's on a rampage." Eileen kept the church organized. She was the senior pastor's secretary and my friend. I occupied the bottom tier of the pastoral food chain as a lowly youth pastor. Larry, one of two retired men who served as volunteer janitors, told Eileen he was looking for me. Eileen gave me the head's up.

Larry was a jovial, but sometimes crabby, and always-outspoken senior citizen. I was a sincere, easily intimidated, 23-year old. My youth group had grown from 30 to almost 200 teenagers who ran amok through our church on Friday nights. I'll admit it was chaos, but it was fun chaos. Okay, it was mildly destructive chaos.

Hence, Larry's rampage. He was committed to keeping the building clean. I was committed to keeping it full of riotous, church-phobic young people. We both held valid commitments. We both wanted to steward God's resources. I'm not saying he was wrong and I was right; I'm just saying we were about to butt heads.

Though he was wrong and I was right.

I've always avoided head-butting. I have the Peace Gene—I crave the absence of conflict. But that day, I'd had enough. I didn't want to hear about how the kids busted a light fixture or left a mess in the sanctuary. My job was to fill the place; Larry's job was to clean the place. No more Mr. Nice Guy!

I gulped and told Eileen, "Well, Larry better watch out for me, because now I'm on a rampage."

Guess who picked that moment to walk into Eileen's office. I knew because Eileen's eyes grew big.

I spun around, got in Larry's face, and spoke in staccato monosyllables, "The next time you have a gripe, tell me first. Don't whine to her." Then, I pulled a power play I'd heard about in college: I moved close enough to plant my right foot between Larry's feet. Let's call this invading his private space. "I'm here to fill this church. You're here to keep it clean. Let me do my job, and I'll let you do yours. Got that?"

I stood there, nose to nose, my leg in his space, staring him down. I felt like David facing Goliath. The color drained from his face, and for the first time in anybody's memory, he didn't know what to say. He stammered a little and said, "Well, uhh, sure. I'm sorry, Bill."

"Fine," I said, backing off. I turned away from him, only to see Eileen's eyes bulging from their sockets. After Larry walked off, she did a silent cheer.

So did I.

I guess I had more power than I thought I did.

So does every child of God. So did Esther. We just have to learn how to use it. Rising above OPC depends on it. Every time we respond to OPC, we'll either use, abuse, be abused by, or run away from somebody's power.

In a brilliant, almost comical, scene, the Author gathers Esther, Haman, and Xerxes in one room for a case study on power. Xerxes epitomizes weakling power—a passive brand of craziness that makes room for evil and fritters life away by degrees. Haman illustrates tyrant power—a needlessly aggressive craziness that claws past others on its climb to the top. Though she comes last to the table of royalty, only Esther exemplifies noble power—she becomes the center of influence and uses her power for a righteous cause.

Let's watch.

Noble Power: Esther

Three days later, Esther put on her royal robes and entered the inner court of the palace, just across from the king's hall. The king was sitting on his royal throne, facing the entrance. (Esther 5:1)

I love the way the Storyteller puts it. She literally writes, "Esther put on royalty." "Robes" isn't in the original; it's an interpolation. Before she risks her life to save her friends, Esther puts on royalty.

As an American, my heart doesn't beat with the tune of royalty. My closest brush with it was as a kid, handling my mom's old Elvis albums. So it's hard for me to relate to royalty. But it's not hard to relate to power or the lack of it.

When Esther "put on royalty" she got in touch with her God-given power. And that is God's desire for you in this OPC-crammed world.

When God created us, he made us in his own image. He gave us a tiny sliver of his infinite sovereignty. The essence of royalty is *wanting* and *willing*. Kings and Queens want what they want and feel entitled to say so. True royalty means discovering what you really want and going after it with all your strength in ways that support others in their quest for royalty too.

When you access your God-given royalty, you won't feel listless or bored. You'll feel real energy. You'll forge connections with others. You'll make sacrifices and hardly realize it. You'll be doing what you love, and nobody will have to drag you out of bed in the morning.

The problem with most of us is not that we're powerless; it's that we don't know what we really want. And because we don't know what we really want, we dabble in a million things instead of jumping wholeheartedly into the focused commitments that will bring the most joy. We shoot buckshot, not bullets.

Or, in those rare cases when we do know what we really want, we're often too intimidated by obstacles to actually pursue it. "The lazy person is full of excuses, saying, 'If I go outside, I might meet a lion in the street and be killed!'" (Proverbs 22:13).

True royals know what they really want, aren't embarrassed to say what they want, and figure out ways to pursue what they want, even if they don't get it.

Wanting and willing.

Christians urgently need to get a grip on this truth. So many of us have been taught that following Jesus means doing the opposite of what we really want. As if, discipleship means living a semi-miserable life till Jesus returns. Too often, we labor under the misconception that doing God's will involves, by definition, a lifestyle of morose, self-denigrating sacrifice, guaranteed to make us look like lemon-sucking victims of our Higher Power.

Do you know how God steers you into doing his will? Through your wants. He puts his wants into your heart, and then summons you forward. There's a catch, though. You have to be following him sincerely—not perfectly—but authentically, or else your flesh will dominate your wants. King David promised, "Take delight in the LORD, and he will give you your heart's desires" (Psalm 37:4).

If God is giving you your heart's desires, it's safe to pursue those desires, right? On the basis of God's Word, I hereby give you permission to discover what you really want, and then apply all your God-given power in that direction. That is noble power. That is real power. That is Esther.

On one level, Esther wanted to hide in the palace, keep a low profile, enjoy her position and wealth, and ignore her people's plight. But that would have been a very boring, very depressing, zombie-ish life.

On a much deeper level, Esther really wanted something else. She wanted the energized life you can only have when you put on royalty to save life and take a risk that looks like it could kill you. The gut-wrenching choice she made proved it.

> When he saw Queen Esther standing there in the inner court, he welcomed her holding out the gold scepter to her. So Esther approached and touched its tip. Then the king asked her, "What do you want, Queen Esther? What is your request? I will give it to you, even if it is half the kingdom!" And Esther replied, "If it please Your Majesty, let the king and Haman come today to a banquet I have prepared for the king." (Esther 5:2-4)

Sometimes, the big scary monster staring you in the face turns out to be a dead bug on the windshield. So Esther shows up, majestic inside and out. Without fanfare, King Xerxes welcomes her.

Or, literally, "she found grace in his sight." And that grace brings her into contact with the royal scepter. And that grace also gains her an extravagant offer from King Xerxes: anything you want, up to half the kingdom.

She didn't have to say a word. She didn't have to make a case, argue the merits, prove her worth, debate the opposition, push through obstacles, answer objections, be quick on her feet, or dodge a barrage of OPC.

She just had to show up.

Problem solved, just by showing up.

All that anxiety. All that hand-wringing. All that delay.

Wasted.

God's grace, special delivery, via a pagan king, was waiting for her to just show up.

What wasn't wasted, however, was her faith. Every step of faith. Every tough choice. Every self-sacrificing breakthrough. When we start showing faith, God starts unleashing grace. Actually, the grace was always there, waiting—like dinner in the oven—and faith is how we come home and dig in (see Isaiah 30:18).

A lot of people, like the king, have authority, power and privilege. But their power doesn't flow from within; it's an external accident of position. The worst OPC spews forth from rulers who are externally powerful but internally weak. Like your ex-boss. Or a dictatorial teacher. Or a nutcase husband or wife or mom or dad. Or a pastor (no "amens" please). Like the king. Like Haman.

But Esther got in touch with her inner power first, and that qualified her to exercise outward power, second. This is what I mean by Noble power.

Noble power makes us shrewd and wise. It provides internal order and structure. It enables us to know what we really want. It leads us into purposeful action. Noble power enables us to sacrifice our lives for a transcendent cause, without a self-destructive, self-denigrating motivation. It is the power that makes moms and dads get up in the middle of the night, without complaint, to feed the baby. It is the power that engages in healthy conflict and doesn't pout when you don't get your way. It is the power to take No for an answer without giving up your dreams.

Noble power makes us humming generators of grace, not of craziness.

When we put on royalty, we can enter crazy situations and not freak out. We can keep our minds, think, analyze, and act in the most stressful environments. Noble power is tactical—it understands how to dance around the crazy king's fragile ego and his advisor's diabolical intent. It can cut through other people's craziness, and make good things happen.

When you get in touch with your God-given noble power, you will become like the sun: others adjust their orbits to you. Esther is just beginning to flex her muscle, so she's shaky. But even as a rookie, her results are spectacular—the king grants her any request up to half the kingdom.

So what kind of power has the king tapped into?

Weakling Power: King Xerxes

Some time ago, I took my happy family to Disneyworld. The Disneyworld staff welcomed us with a boatload of passive-OPC. We parked our rental car, unloaded our exuberant kids and gathered our cameras. I asked a nearby parking attendant where to wait for the tram. He pointed to an area marked out on the pavement. We were the first giddy, happy family there. The attendant waved at us and smiled. Others saw us standing there, and figured we were in the right spot, so they joined us. Our numbers quickly swelled to a couple dozen eager visitors to the Magic Kingdom.

It didn't take long for the magic to fade.

A tram came our way, but just kept going. It drove right by us. We were close enough to touch it, but it didn't stop. That's okay, we figured. It was half full. Maybe an emptier tram was coming.

Other families joined our clueless throng. The group grew to fifty people. Only yards away, Disney "cast members" continued guiding cars to their parking spaces. People continued to join our group, waiting for a tram.

A second tram came by. Loaded with people, but by no means full. It too, just kept going, right past us.

Close to 100 people were by then milling around. We had waited fifteen minutes. We were confused and hot and irritated. Our young kids melted down into impatient whiners, "When is the tram coming?"

Finally, I jogged over to a parking attendant—not the first one who guided us to our spot, but a different one. "When's the tram coming?" I asked. "We've been passed up by several of them."

"You guys shouldn't be waiting there; that's not a tram stop. You can actually walk from here—you don't even need a tram. The main entrance is around the turn by those flags." He pointed just a few yards away.

Aaaarrrgggghhhh! Those parking attendants watched us mill around for fifteen minutes and said nothing. They were fewer than 25 yards away from us. They could have taken some initiative and told us to just keep walking. But no. They let us stand there and start our visit with a sour taste in our mouths.

We were victims of passive OPC.

We collected our kids and walked. In my head, I composed the blistering letter I would write to any Disney family member still living. In the end, I decided to just let it go and have a good time.

Passive craziness abdicates its own power. It represents a flight from power. It manifests itself whenever people are dependent, chronically needy, lazy, weak-willed, indecisive, and don't get the job done. God gave you your power to bless yourself by blessing others. That is true nobility. That is what the Disney parking attendants failed to display. And that is exactly the opposite of Xerxes' spirit.

Esther bumps into the king's passive OPC and to save lives, she exploits his passivity to the max. She starts by hosting a cozy wine-tasting party for Xerxes and Haman.

> The king turned to his attendants and said, "Tell Haman to come quickly to a banquet, as Esther has requested." So the king and Haman went to Esther's banquet. And while they were drinking wine, the king said to Esther, "Now tell me what you really want. What is your request? I will give it to you, even if it is half the kingdom!" Esther replied, "This is my request and deepest wish. If Your Majesty is pleased with me and wants to grant my request, please come with Haman tomorrow to the banquet I will prepare for you. Then tomorrow I will explain what this is all about." (Esther 5:5-8)

Xerxes exhibits three classic symptoms of passive sovereignty.

1. Impulsive. Esther extends her invitation, and like a schoolboy with a crush, Xerxes can't wait. He commands Haman to come running, and off they go.

In a university study, researchers tempted four-year-olds with a marshmallow. They told the kids that they could either eat one marshmallow right away, or wait twenty minutes and enjoy two marshmallows. The researchers tracked the kids over time, and discovered that those who delayed their marshmallow gratification at age four did better in school, were better adjusted in adolescence, and scored 210 points higher on standardized testing than their impulsive counterparts.[4]

2. Outlandish. Xerxes offers Esther half the kingdom. That's nice, King, but it's a bit crazy, don't you think?

This is the guilty parent buying the expensive sports car for the surly sixteen year-old. It is the grandiose gesture. The over-the-top promises made to buy love. The ultra-expensive wedding of two half-hearted partners. Noble power is measured and wise. Weakling power tries to shout its worth.

3. Absent. I've peeked ahead to chapter 7, and just when the whole story gets really tense, and Esther tells the king about Haman's evil plot, and it's the perfect time for him to be a man, he stands up and leaves the room (Esther 7:7). Just like fathers who leave their families or shopaholics who ignore their credit card bills or students who neglect their studies. Weaklings deal with stress by absenting themselves.

Notice how Esther treats the king at their little wine-tasting. She doesn't tell him her request, yet. She postpones him. Maybe Esther knows that passive OPC is fickle and impulsive, so she wants to get him hyped up before he'll make the right decision and actually follow through. She also knows that Haman is shrewd. Fortunately, she's shrewder.

You might call Esther's approach noble manipulation. Jesus calls it being "wise as serpents" (Matthew 10:16). Xerxes is a puppet, and to save life, Esther will shamelessly pull his strings. That's how she deals with OPC—the passive kind. She is wise, patient, and tactical.

121

We should follow her steps. We will always have passive crazies in our life: those who shirk responsibility, avoid mental work, or postpone important decisions. Procrastinators. Slackers. Weasels. Wimps.

God loves them, and we're stuck loving them too—or at least working with them.

They are driven by insecurity and/or laziness. They're out of touch with their own power. They have few priorities in life beside what feels good in the moment. Whatever is happening right now sets the agenda. Like Xerxes, they connive others into pampering them. They buy love with favors, but can't commit. They're paralyzed with indecision. They always have somebody to blame. They have no shortage of ready-made excuses for their dull, bland, waste of a perfectly good life. They are perpetual victims.

They want you to make decisions for them. And when you're weak, you do.

Esther reveals the core secret of dealing with passive OPC: Never let weaklings drag you down to their limp level. We might be tempted to fly low to keep from embarrassing them. Forget it, I say. Embarrass their itty-bitty souls with impunity. Just because they've chosen a small life with a small god doesn't mean you have to shrink to make them feel better about themselves. If your courage highlights their cowardice, great. If your productivity shows up their ineffectiveness, do it. They need it. You do nobody any favors by playing dumb or flying low.

You have to be careful though; there's nothing more dangerous than a wimp who turns violent.

Enter Haman.

Tyrant Power: Haman

What a happy man Haman was as he left the banquet! But when he saw Mordecai sitting at the gate, not standing up or trembling nervously before him, he was furious. (Esther 5:9)

In the neighborhood where I grew up, a mass murderer targeted teenage boys and buried their bodies in his basement. I rode my bike past that house many times and never suspected a thing. Compounding the fear-factor, the killer moonlighted as a party rent-a-clown. The news stunned the community.

This guy had been everybody's friend. (Not mine; my family had never met him.) Apparently, the nicest man on the block.

Now, an army of investigators excavated his basement-turned-graveyard, unearthing body after body. Thirty-three in all. Jovial and laughing one minute; murderously depraved the next. He switched back and forth from Friendly Neighbor to Homicidal Maniac in a flash.

Like Haman. He leaves the party with joy in his heart. It pops like a balloon the moment he sees Mordecai. Haman is the second most powerful man in the kingdom, he has just had a private wine tasting with the king and queen, he got his way to kill all the Jews in just eleven months, and he's still not satisfied.

Haman represents raw tyrant-power. While the king displays passive craziness, Haman displays aggressive craziness. In a rage, Haman stomps home, and gathers his household to regale them with his glories:

However, he restrained himself and went on home. Then he gathered together his friends and Zeresh, his wife, and boasted to them about his great wealth and his many children. He bragged about the honors the king had given him and how he had been promoted over all the other officials and leaders. Then Haman added, "And that's not all! Queen Esther invited only me and the king himself to the banquet she prepared for us. And she has invited me to dine with her and the king again tomorrow!"

Then he added, "But all this is meaningless as long as I see Mordecai the Jew just sitting there at the palace gate." (Esther 5:10-13)

Tyrant-Power Rule 1: The people in my life are props to support my fragile sense of importance.

Tyrant-Power Rule 2: I must destroy anyone who won't play along with rule one.

Haman proves that a tyrannical soul can never be satisfied. No amount of wealth, prestige, power, comfort, pleasure, caving in, or wimping out—nothing will satisfy that soul until it eliminates a scapegoat. If you're the scapegoat, keep your shields up and your mind alert. Abuse is one kind of OPC you can't manage. You have to get out. Negotiate or reconcile or break it off from a safe distance only.

Unfortunately, Esther doesn't have that option. So she pursues another option. But that has to wait for two chapters.

If you find yourself more like Haman, beware. There is no excuse for bullying. There is no excuse for inflicting harm—emotional, physical, spiritual, or mental—on anybody for any reason. I get that "hurt people hurt people" but that's an observation, not a rationalization. If your life casts the shadow of Haman, please get the help you need before you cross lines you promised you'd never cross. Even if you've already crossed those lines, with God's help, there's always a way out.

Notice the advice Haman receives from his sweetie-pie, Zeresh:

> So Haman's wife, Zeresh, and all his friends suggested, "Set up a gallows that stands seventy-five feet tall, and in the morning ask the king to hang Mordecai on it. When this is done, you can go on your merry way to the banquet with the king." This pleased Haman immensely, and he ordered the gallows set up. (Esther 5:14)

How creepy is she! They're a matched set. The Bible says, "The king's fury is like a lion's roar; to rouse his anger is to risk your life" (Proverbs 20:2). To Haman and Zeresh, people are objects just waiting to be exploited.

Some experts suggest that by hanging, Zeresh actually meant spiking. Ancient Persians impaled their victims on gigantic spikes and mounted the spikes like telephone poles, leaving the wretched victim to wiggle to death up on top.

Tyrants tip their hand in six ways:

1. They can't be pleased. They easily find something to complain about. The boatload of misery in your relationship is all your fault.

2. They throw tantrums, pout, or fly into a rage. They curse, throws stuff, and utter threats. They don't hide their cruelty. Sometimes.

3. Other times, they hide their cruelty. Their actions don't warrant contacting authorities, but you've thought about it. They deliver underhanded jabs, hurtful one-liners, sarcasm, and a host of demeaning facial expressions. Sometimes, they're so subtle, they've convinced themselves and you they're not cruel.

4. They suffer an incredible need to be noticed. They obsess over image and aren't happy with anything second-best in their lives. Even though they can't afford it.

5. They treat you as an object to meet their needs. You're the trophy wife, the sugar daddy, or the boy-toy. When they want to use you, they'll make you feel like the Ruler of the World. When the tyrant has had his way with you, he'll throw you overboard in a heartbeat.

6. They control you. How you dress, speak, look, arrange the house, spend your free time, and cut your hair. A tyrant won't be satisfied till everyone bows. Global domination.

The chapter begins and ends with Happy Haman. It starts happy because of his private tête-à-tête with the king and queen. It ends happy because of his Zeresh-inspired plan to spike Mordecai. The crazies around you play the power-game for keeps. Their happiness depends on it. Like Esther, your happiness—and sometimes your survival—depends on your willingness to flex your muscle too.

Sometimes, evil prevails. Sometimes, the mass murderer, the genocidal maniac, the abuser, or the Haman next door, gains the upper hand. As Christians, we see that as temporary. Our world is fallen; its wounds bleed from a self-invited cosmic curse. Yet that falleness doesn't get the final say. Hopefully, Haman won't get the final say in Esther. We'll see.

But we can be sure of one thing: Sometimes the Unseen God flexes his muscle in ways nobody saw coming. Never forget the Divine power—righteous, holy, and good—hiding in the shadows of every other power.

𒐀 𒐗 𒈨 𒌋 𒐀 ⤙

Reflections

Reflections 1: Fill in this blank: when I feel really stressed, I get really _____.

For you, does that blank most resemble Esther, Haman, or Xerxes? When God made you, he gave you power. It's as if he poured a thimbleful of his own omnipotence and sovereignty into you. The Bible says that God made us masters over his creation and told us to exercise dominion (Genesis 1:28). Paul writes that Christ's followers shall "reign in life" (Romans 5:17, NKJV).

God designed you to flex your muscle. He gave you power and wants you to use it. One way or another, you will use it. The only question is how. Will you use your power in a noble way, a weakling way, or a tyrannical way?

The best way to identify how you use your power is by observing yourself in times of stress. Adversity brings out both the best and the worst in us. So, how do you handle stress? When you're sleep-deprived. When responsibilities overwhelm you. When you're confused and frightened. When the money runs low. When the doctor sounds worried. When the kids wear you out. When you feel dumb. When you look foolish. In those cases, how do you use your power?

Be honest. Fill in this blank: when I feel really stressed, I get really _____. Fill in multiple answers if you need to. Ask a friend or spouse or loved one to help you. You might be surprised. On second thought, don't ask them to help you— you might go "Zeresh" on them if you don't like their answers.

How about some suggestions? Just highlight all that apply: when I feel stressed, I get... nasty, mean, sullen, pouty, loud, violent, self-pitying, sarcastic, hostile, hungry, tired, vicious, thoughtful, calm, forgiving, vengeful, quiet, wimpy, compliant, self-denigrating, self-sacrificing, clingy, needy, dependent, scared, anxious, withdrawn, rebellious, drunk, high, stoned, buzzed, solitary, snappish, scathing, attacking, rude, vulgar, catty, gossipy, selfish, spiteful, controlling, bitchy, sissified, spiteful, cruel, harsh, bitter, angry, pathetic, confused, lost, helpless, vindictive, busy, distracted, funny, joking, clownish, prayerful, worshipful, analytical, solution-oriented, peaceful, steady, fickle, vacillating, compassionate, godly, relational, caring, trusting, loving.

Okay, never mind. I forgot. I'm not supposed to put you on the hot seat. I'm sorry. Skip this Reflections.

Reflections 2: When you face passive craziness keep your dignity and be shrewd.

The Bible says: "Whoever has no rule over his own spirit is like a city broken down, without walls" (Proverbs 25:28, NKJV). The English word, integrity, comes from a Latin root that means *untouched*. Picture a city under attack with no breach in the walls. The occupants remain untouched. Integrity means not letting OPC rule you. You rule, not the crazies out there. Keep your dignity. Rule your spirit. Stay poised, even if you're stuck sipping wine with the neighborhood weakling and the local bully.

Reflections 3: When you face aggressive craziness, take your stand and quit bowing, but make yourself safe first, if you can.

Mordecai and Esther were cut from the same cloth. They both flexed their muscle; they both refused to bow. Notice that

Mordecai's courage seemed natural. It came from within. Nobody talked him into it. But Esther's courage seemed coached. Mordecai talked her through it. She psyched herself up for it.

I love that part of the story. It gives me hope. For all of those times my gut reaction is fear and my instinct tells me to run, there's still hope. Even if I have to psyche myself into courage, and even if I'm trembling all the way to the conflict, it's okay.

Courage isn't the absence of fear; it's action in the face of fear. What does God's power feel like when it flows through us? Trembly. Paul said, "I came to you in weakness—timid and trembling" (1 Corinthians 2:3)—a confession that pretty much sums up my life.

Many Christians labor under the delusion that we have to feel powerful or else we're defective Christians. No. You don't have to *feel* powerful. It's nice when you do, but for the follower of Jesus, it's optional. God doesn't require that you feel powerful, at least not all the time. He intends that you make powerful choices even when you feel inadequate. His "strength is made perfect in [your] weakness" (2 Corinthians 12:9). That's why I love Esther. She's rising above OPC, even though she's scared out of her wits. Let's rise above OPC too.

FOR DISCUSSION AND REFLECTION: How does your culture and group feel about weakness? How do you feel? What has your spiritual journey taught you about weakness and strength? Have you ever had a problem that just solved itself? How did grace play into the process? Describe some times when you've seen passive OPC, dangerous OPC, and noble OPC in action.

𝍥 𝍦 𝍧 𝍨 𝍥 𝍩

There is another place where the Bible throws weakling power, tyrant power, and noble power into one room. See if you can identify them:

> Therefore, when the chief priests and officers saw Him, they cried out, saying, "Crucify Him, crucify Him!" Then Pilate said to Him, "...[D]o You not know that I have power to crucify You, and power to release You?" Jesus answered, "You could have no power at all against Me unless it had been given you from above..." (John 19:6,10,11, NKJV)

Who displayed Weakling power? Pilate.

Who displayed Tyrant power? The chief priests and officers.

Who displayed Royal power? Jesus! Imagine him looking Pilate in the eye. Jesus is bloodied. Beaten. By the looks of it, utterly defeated. But he rises up like true royalty, looks Pilate in the eye, and tells him he has no power at all but what had been given him by somebody else. There is the true king! There is the champion! Can anybody overpower the power of Jesus? It might look like it, but it can never happen.

Thomas Edison patented his light bulb in 1878. Question: when was there more electricity in the world? Five hundred years ago, or today? The answer is neither. The clouds of the sky, and the electrons of every atom have always held within them all the electricity there ever will be. The power has always been there. Our problem was never the absence of electricity. Our problem has been that we have not learned how to harness that power.

Jesus Christ has stored up within him all the power of God. And if you are a Christian, you have Jesus living in you.

For much of your life, perhaps, you have tried to live by your own power. You have tried to solve the problems of Other People's Craziness. You have tried to find your true calling and galvanize your life.

And, because you do it by your own power, you are tired, confused, weary, and frustrated. Maybe you have even given up. You have slipped into tyrant power, or weakling power over and over. But all along, Jesus has been saying, "You have no power at all except what I have given you. Use my power."

But you don't know how.

Do you want to know how?

Keep reading.

CHAPTER 9

Leave Room for God

ID YOU EVER HAVE A PROBLEM that solved itself? In the Bible, the classic case was the parting of the Red Sea. A vengeance-driven Pharaoh and his invincible army rode hard after the Jews. Their mission was to capture them and return them to a depressingly servile life. The Jews had nowhere to run; they were blocked by the Red Sea. Yet before their very eyes, God sent a great wind and parted the sea. Problem solved. By itself. They just stood there.

In another case, a dedicated follower of God named Daniel faced a serious problem. Daniel's weakling king had just ordered him tossed, head over heels, into a den of ravenous, man-eating lions. We might call this a very big problem. Imagine Daniel's wonderment, however, when the lions approached him—not menacingly and not stalkingly—not to eat him, but to nuzzle him. To purr. To roll over so Daniel could pet their soft tummies. God sent his angel and shut the lions' mouths. Problem solved. Daniel just stood there.

I had a boss tell me, "Either you come into work right now or don't bother coming back at all." I was 19 years old, working as a produce clerk in a large grocery store. On the day the manager hired me, I told them I couldn't work on Tuesday nights because I ran a boys' club at my church. The manager accepted that condition and hired me. Three weeks into the job, he put me on the schedule to work on Tuesday night. I reminded him that I couldn't come in, and he agreed to change the schedule.

Then he forgot.

Tuesday came. At home, sporting my kids-club uniform, I was heading out the door when the phone rang. "Bill, where are you? You're late!" my boss said.

I reminded him that he had agreed to change the schedule. He didn't remember, and told me to come in. I refused. Then he said, "Either you come into work right now or don't bother coming back at all." I told him, "I'm sorry, but there are 40 kids waiting for me, and they're more important than this job."

Long silence.

"I want to talk to you tomorrow," he said.

I went to my boys' club with the nagging fear that I was about to chalk up the first termination on my young resume.

By nature, I'm a worrier. I worry about money. I worry about health. I worry about the direction of our culture. I worry about my church, my family, my kids. I worry about how long I can nurse two cars along with over 110,000 miles each. I'm a worrier from a long line of worriers.

So, my late teenage self worried over what my boss would say. I rehearsed my arguments. I prepared my case. I thought through all the scenarios. I calculated how to regain his favor. I fussed and stressed. And, oh yes, I actually prayed and asked my friends to pray. I planned a multi-pronged strategy to persuade my boss not to fire me.

My hopes, however, were not high.

The next day came. I white-knuckled my drive to work, gulped, and walked on wobbly legs to meet my employer. I inhaled to launch my meticulously planned speech, but he beat me to it.

"Bill, as far as I'm concerned, nothing happened last night."

That was it.

I just stood there. Problem solved, all by itself. Or maybe, I should say, all by God's Self. And they never scheduled me on Tuesday night again.

I'm not saying this happens every time.

Many times—most times—our problems do not solve themselves. But sometimes they do, and there are reasons for it. That's what happens in Esther 6.

A Royal Case of Insomnia

That night the king had trouble sleeping, so he ordered an attendant to bring the historical records of his kingdom so they could be read to him. In those records he discovered an account of how Mordecai had exposed the plot of Bigthana and Teresh, two of the eunuchs who guarded the door to the king's private quarters. They had plotted to assassinate the king. "What reward or recognition did we ever give Mordecai for this?" the king asked. His attendants replied, "Nothing has been done." (Esther 6:1-3)

Royal insomnia triggers every event in this chapter. Not Esther's effort. Not Mordecai's faithfulness. Not even the fasting and prayer of the Jews, though that may be an indirect cause. The Author, however, allows the king's insomnia to trigger a chain reaction that alters global history. Why?

Why after all Esther's courage, and Mordecai's prodding, and the Jews praying—why do the efforts of the key players suddenly recede? Esther and Mordecai lie nestled snug in their beds, but the king can't sleep. And without either Esther or Mordecai or the Jews lifting even one little finger, all of a sudden, the most evil man in a generation gets a bull's-eye painted on his heart, and the divine Avenger draws back his bow.

Why?

That's the question the Author wants us to consider.

Call it irony, call it coincidence, call it God's sense of humor, call it Providence, but at the very moment the king wishes to heap gratitude on Mordecai, guess who's knocking on his door to ask permission to hang Mordecai.

A Shock to the System

"Who is that in the outer court?" the king inquired. Now, as it happened, Haman had just arrived in the outer court of the palace to ask the king to hang Mordecai from the gallows he had prepared. So the attendants replied to the king, "Haman is out there." "Bring him in," the king ordered. (Esther 6:4, 5)

Haman is about to receive the shock of a lifetime. For three chapters in a row, he has been the driving force behind every paragraph. The whole story revolves around his diabolical craziness. He likes it that way. He feels like the sun, and everyone else is just a planetoid orbiting his gravity.

But here, Haman receives a shock to the system. He discovers he is not the center of the universe.

It's funny because Haman is such a self-absorbed jerk, that even when the king summons him to honor Mordecai, Haman thinks the king wants to honor him. So we read with growing amusement as the king's real intentions unfold.

The storyteller stacks up coincidences: Haman completes his gallows on the very same night the king can't sleep. When the king's bedtime readers open his journals, they just so happen to find the place where Mordecai saved the king's life. This happens at the same time Haman lurks outside the king's chambers to ask permission to hang Mordecai. This also happens when the king seeks any available official to honor Mordecai.

Coincidences? Really?

The Author puts flesh on two inviolable laws of reality:

Inviolable Law One: Only God is smart enough to orchestrate the events of your life.

Inviolable Law Two: Only God is strong enough to teach the crazies in your life that the world does not revolve around them.

No human power can weave together the coincidences described here. Yet, somehow it all fits together. What look like random events are actually interlocking parts in a divine Megablock set. A foiled assassination plot triggers Haman's downfall in a way nobody saw coming.

It almost looks as if Somebody up there might be calling the shots.

That neighbor who blasts his car stereo, that aunt who offers unwanted "suggestions" on your home decor, that boss who dumps her work on you at the last minute, that ex- who makes your life a living hell—are they the center of your universe? They may try to be. They may think they are. But do you have to let them be? Haman has been at the center for a long time. And now, just at the right time, the Unseen Hand shoves him to the side, even as it lifts the faithful follower of God to new glory.

Perhaps God has an agenda.

Perhaps he is saying that, though the world seems crazy now, in an ultimate sense, God will permit nobody to supplant Jesus from his rightful throne. And there's no OPC that can thwart him.

From the first to the last page of Scripture, God has balanced the cosmos on the Lord Jesus Christ. He is the King of kings and Lord of Lords. He is the shepherd of the stars and the fascination of the angels. He is the One at whose feet every knee shall bow.

A day is coming when God will arrange the whole universe under the authority of Christ (Ephesians 1:10). Every wiggling atom, every complex molecule, every bit of energy, every person, place and thing, every craziness, every abuser, every angel, every demon, every thought, every prayer, every dream, every sinner, every saint, every sin, and every righteousness—everything and everyone will be placed in their proper orbit in relation to the True Center. And that center will not be Haman or any crazy person in your life.

That center will be Jesus.

Consider the center *occupied*.

And know that God promises any usurper a sure and certain crash and burn. It's just a matter of time.

God cares immensely about the OPC you face.

The Bible discloses that when Jesus entered heaven, God pulled up a plush recliner and told him: "Sit at my right hand, Son, until I make your enemies a footstool for your feet" (Psalm 110:1; Hebrews 1:13). Today, it's Haman's turn. And the people who torment you stand in the same line as Haman. It's only a matter of time.

If you are God's child, God takes OPC against you personally. God is not only gracious, he is also righteously dangerous.

So Haman stalls and begins his death spiral. In one short chapter, his carcass will provide a tasty treat for maggots.

An Ultimate Solution

> So Haman came in, and the king said, "What should I do to honor a man who truly pleases me?" Haman thought to himself, "Whom would the king wish to honor more than me?" So he replied, "If the king wishes to honor someone, he should bring out one of the king's own royal robes, as well as the king's own horse with a royal emblem on its head. Instruct one of the king's most noble princes to dress the man in the king's robe and to lead him through the city square on the king's own horse. Have the prince shout as they go, 'This is what happens to those the king wishes to honor!'" (Esther 6:6-9)

The original sin is pride, and it came to life in Lucifer's heart. It scurried into Adam and Eve, and infected us all. Pride is the mother of all sins, nurturing within its womb its own brood of OPC gremlins.

> Pride goes before destruction, / And a haughty spirit before a fall. (Proverbs 16:18, NKJV)

Scripture encourages healthy pride. I take huge satisfaction in my wife and kids. I'm proud of my family. I'm proud of my church. I'm proud of the man I've become. I'm proud of a lot of things, in a healthy way.

I hope you're proud of yourself, too. Proud of surviving. Proud of lasting this long. Proud of what you see in the mirror, even though none of us is perfect. Healthy pride—an inner satisfaction in your God given identity and grace-empowered achievements—is a very good thing.

Destructive pride, however, is a monster. It feeds on other people's weaknesses. It mocks their losses. It condemns their foibles. It turns people into bullies or mean girls. It puts others on edge, and makes people close to you walk on eggshells.

Call it arrogance. Call it cockiness. Call it hubris. Destructive pride masks deep insecurities that can only be healed by an encounter with the grace of God.

God designed you for honor and respect. He made you to receive dignity. You are created for glory.

But only God can give it.

God alone can bestow the deep-rooted honor that you crave. He is orchestrating your life's events to fill your heart with his love. As a sacrificial lamb, Jesus absorbed the world's craziness that we might be filled with God's glory.

But Haman looked to a different sacrificial lamb to find his honor. His deluded brain wonders, "Whom would the king wish to honor more than me?" The Hebrew phrase, "more than" is a rare combination of words that indicates extreme excessiveness. Haman reasons, "There is no one who has ever lived in all the human race who is even a fraction as wonderful as me!"

Epic conceit.

Plus, remember why Haman lurked at the king's door in the first place: he wanted permission to spike Mordecai. So words cannot describe the jolt that Haman felt when the king dropped the bombshell of verse ten.

Not A Special Snowflake

"Excellent!" the king said to Haman. "Hurry and get the robe and my horse, and do just as you have said for Mordecai the Jew, who sits at the gate of the palace. Do not fail to carry out everything you have suggested." (Esther 6:10)

We can probably express Haman's feeling in five words: "I am going to puke." If this were anybody other than a wannabe mass murderer, we'd feel sorry for him.

This might be a very good time to ask, *where was Esther while all this happened?* Where was Mordecai? Where were the Jews? Here, the great enemy of God's people, begins his fall. And how much help did God need here? His principal agents aren't even in the picture. It might turn out that grace— God working by his own power, without our help—might be the ultimate undoing of OPC.

So Haman took the robe and put it on Mordecai, placed him on the king's own horse, and led him through the city square, shouting, "This is what happens to those the king wishes to honor!" Afterward Mordecai returned to the palace gate, but Haman hurried home dejected and completely humiliated. When Haman told his wife, Zeresh, and all his friends what had happened, they said, "Since Mordecai—this man who has humiliated you—is a Jew, you will never succeed in your plans against him. It will be fatal to continue to oppose him." While they were still talking, the king's eunuchs arrived to take Haman to the banquet Esther had prepared." (Esther 6:11-14)

Haman has just gagged on the first mouthful off his own craziness. There might be more gagging ahead.

Though dejected and humiliated, Haman still has it better than the Jews he wants to slaughter. So what? He still feels sorry for himself. I love his wife's cheery evaluation: "Since Mordecai... is a Jew, you will never succeed in your plans against him. It will be fatal to continue to oppose him."

Too bad he didn't listen to her. She's smarter than him.

Grace

This part of the story makes me feel sinisterly gleeful. Haman has triggered his self-destruct sequence. Haman, who was calling all the shots. Haman, with his bloodlust against the Jews. Haman, who was the king's best friend and top advisor. This giant of a man, with all his power, fame, wealth, and prestige—with all his insider influence, this gargantuan craziness in Esther's life—has been pushed onto a pirate's plank, and is about to be shoved off the end.

And who did it?

Not Esther. Not Mordecai. They make nothing happen here. Esther doesn't even warrant a mention in this chapter.

And yet, back in the harem, her young shoulders slump under the hulking burden of salvation for the Jews. She is utterly clueless that tonight, an Unnamed Somebody has set the table for her victory tomorrow. An Unnamed Somebody makes this salvation happen all by his own power, without one bit of help from Esther.

That is the grace of God—without your help, your assistance, your good works, your anything. In grace's realm, God gives and we receive. It's that simple.

What is grace? A.W. Tozer said, "Grace is the good pleasure of God that inclines Him to bestow benefits upon the undeserving."[5] B.B. Warfield kicked it up a notch: "Grace is very distinctly and very emphatically love to the ill-deserving."[6] John Piper adds a whole new dimension, "Grace is power, not just pardon."[7]

Grace is the power of God doing for us what we could never do for ourselves, all on the basis of Christ and his Cross.

We are saved by grace—Jesus, by his death and resurrection, accomplished all the work required to reconcile us to God. And we live by grace too—Jesus, through his indwelling power, enables us to walk in his steps. Yes, we must act and strive. But we act through faith by the power of God, so that even our acting and striving spin-off from grace.

The devil scored big points when he flipped Christianity on its head in the minds of the masses. According to the majority perception, Christianity buries its mesmerized disciples under an avalanche of duties: we must follow Jesus, do good works, perform religious rituals, go to church, avoid sin, be conservative, give your money, sacrifice our deepest desires, adopt puritanical values, and stay ten steps behind the modern world. To an on-looking world, Christianity appears as just another variation of the age-old religious theme.

As if the core of Christianity is our works for God.

But the world has it backwards—and the devil is laughing up his sleeve. Christianity is God's work for us through Christ. Jesus and his singular, self-giving, other-loving, sacrificial work occupies the center. The great bulk of the Bible revels in God's commitment to you, not your commitment to God. The Christian message highlights God's love for you, his sacrifice for you, and his ceaseless efforts on your behalf. The Bible is not principally a compendium of things you should do for God (works), but of things God has done for you in Christ (grace) and will do through you through an indwelling Christ (grace)—the outcome of which is your good works some day in the future (also a function of grace, Ephesians 2:10).

Christ's sacrificial death was so effective in cleansing our sins, that if you put down this book, and committed some heinous sin—and if you are in Christ—God's love for you will not flicker even one bit. God will not alter his covenant of love

142

in the slightest, and it doesn't matter what you do, or don't do, or how well you follow Jesus or don't follow Jesus. God loves you because of who and what Jesus is, not because of who and what you are. That's what grace means.

Some may think it's scandalous that I wrote that.

Christianity stands as the one system in all religious history that focuses on what God has done without one bit of help from you. And the second you flip that over, the devil smiles. It's not about you. You're not even in the room. It's about God and Jesus through his honest-to-goodness amazing grace.

The Harder You Try the Worse You Feel

Perhaps for much of your life, you have tried hard to be a good person. You discipline yourself. You make good choices. You care about character. You cope with Other People's Craziness. You try hard to be a good Christian. You pray when you can. You read your Bible when you find time. You attend worship services as your schedule allows. And you might even tithe faithfully.

But something gnaws your conscience. When you compare your life to Jesus, you see a gargantuan gap. That gap scolds you, like the indignant teacher who caught you mixing explosives with the chemistry set. Allegedly.

Perhaps, like Esther, you feel a hulking burden weighing you down: Be a good Christian. Handle OPC. Live the WWJD lifestyle. Stop smoking, stop swearing, stop gossiping, stop living in the flesh, stop having affairs, stop sleeping around, click away from the porn, stop worrying about money, quit overeating. Read your Bible and pray every day. Love your neighbor. Love your enemy. Work hard. Be pure. You've accumulated so much baggage that you can barely stay afloat. One misstep and you'll go down like the Titanic.

You are spiritually tired, confused, weary, and frustrated. You're another Esther, back in her apartment, fretting, anxious, praying, agonizing, strategizing, and working so hard—

To make something happen that God has already made happen by his own power—and you won't even find out until it's a done deal.

Grace shifts the burden from your shoulders to God's.

Breathe.

Rest.

Be at peace.

Your salvation has been won.

What does it say about us that we have this insanely stubborn drive to drag our burdens back to ourselves?

It says we're legalists to the core. Hi, my name is Bill. I'm a recovering legalist.

But in one glorious night, when Esther is nowhere to be seen, God does by his own power what Esther could have never done in a lifetime. That's grace.

So go ahead and flex your muscle—but always leave room for God. While you're sleeping, he's working. Problem solved. God looks at his errant child and says, "As far as I'm concerned, nothing happened yesterday." He looks at his needlessly burdened child and says, "Cast your burdens on me."

Amazing grace. Now all you need is the faith to step into it.

Reflections

Reflection 1: Leave room for God in your post-salvation spiritual life.

Most people who call themselves Christians would say they were saved by grace. But what comes after that? Works? Law? Striving?

Not exactly.

An old-time British preacher, F.B. Meyer, described his struggle as a novice Christian: he longed to live as a fully devoted follower of Jesus. He read his Bible, served Jesus, and prayed. He worshipped and got involved in the church. Meyer sincerely sought to do what Jesus would do in every situation in his life.

On one occasion, he took part in a prayer meeting where participants prayed for God's power to follow Christ. The prayer was intense; they weren't just praying, he said. They were "agonizing." They begged God, pleading and striving in prayer to call down the power of God. This went on for hours.

You probably haven't agonized in prayer for hours, but if you've ever longed for a top-quality Christian life, you might identify with F.B. Meyer. He could be the poster child for Christians who have burned themselves out trying to please God.

But, in the middle of that intense prayer time, Meyer made a life-altering discovery. He wrote,

> I was too tired to agonize, and I somehow felt that God did not want me to agonize hour after hour, but I had to learn to take; that God wanted to give, and I had only to take.

Tomorrow your little girl will come down to breakfast. She is very hungry, and the bread and milk or the oatmeal is on the table. You do not say, "Little girlie, run upstairs, and agonize, and roll on the floor for an hour, and then come down." You say to her, "Little one, I am so glad you have got a good appetite. Now there is your chair, in you get, say your prayer, and start away."

So I left that prayer-meeting.... As I walked I said, "Oh my God, if there is a man who needs the power of God to rest upon him it is I; but I do not know how to receive [it]. I am too tired, too worn, too nervously down to agonize."

A voice said to me, "As you took forgiveness from the hand of the dying Christ, take the Holy Ghost from the hand of the living Christ..." By faith, without emotion, without excitement I took, and took for the first time, and I have kept on taking ever since.[9]

Meyer made room for God in his post-salvation spiritual life. Yes, there's room for emotion and excitement in our lives. There is also lots and lots of room for exertion and striving in our struggle for faith. Meyer's point, however, is that God's grace reaches out to unadorned faith, and all the other stuff we might add is superfluous. In fact, it can get in the way. While you're sleeping, God's working.

Grace.

FOR REFLECTION AND DISCUSSION: Read Colossians 2:13-23 and make a list of some of the things that can get in the way of God's grace flowing through you. In your actual experience, who bears the weight of your post-salvation spiritual success? You or God? Who *should* bear that weight? Read Galatians 2:20 and draw another pie chart.

CHAPTER 10

Risking the Life You Have to Gain the Life You Want

WHAT DOES THE FAITHFUL DISCIPLE contribute to the work of God? Technically, nothing but a leap of faith, just like Esther.

Here's a truth that should kick your spiritual maturity up a notch: *faith is a situation-specific shape-shifter.* Learn it well. Sometimes faith requires action, other times inaction. Depending on the situation, faith may require speaking or keeping silent, fighting or laying down arms, waiting or acting, resting or working, asking or not asking again.

Faith is not a one-size-fits-all proposition. It's changeable.

Let that sink in.

𒀭𒍝𒈗𒅗𒊩𒍪

I slammed my hand on the floor, begging for mercy. Tony's chokehold cut off the oxygen supply to my brain. Only his instant release kept me from passing out.

"And that's how you do a rear, carotid chokehold," said Tony. "It pinches the carotid artery. If you hold it long enough, you'll put your opponent to sleep."

Tony was my black-belt instructor in Brazilian Jiu-Jitsu. I was a 30-something white belt, getting tossed around by jiu-jitsu guys like my German shepherd dog tossed around her toy rat. Tony taught, "It's not that you're looking for a fight. It's just that when a fight comes looking for you, you're ready."

I wrote this book because OPC is the fight that comes looking for you every single day.

You can't avoid OPC, so what will you do about it? Will you roll over and play dead, lash out and take revenge, or take your stand like a true Christian soldier and fight the fight of faith? Whether or not you ever reach the abundant life Jesus promised depends on how well you handle OPC.

Handling OPC is a dance with grace and faith. Just when it seems as if evil will destroy everything, and just when the responsibility is too much to bear, God swoops in to do by his power what we could never do by ours. That's grace. Then we step into the victory his grace has provided day by day. That's faith.

Esther is about to step into a beautiful showcase of grace right now. As Haman babbles incoherently about how quickly his life has turned bad, the guards come to escort him to the second wine tasting with Queen Esther.

It's time for fireworks.

An Offer You Can't Refuse

> So the king and Haman went to Queen Esther's banquet. And while they were drinking wine that day, the king again asked her, "Tell me what you want, Queen Esther. What is your request? I will give it to you, even if it is half the kingdom!" (Esther 7:1, 2)

Consider this an offer Esther can't refuse. This is third time the king has offered this "Offer" to Esther.

Picture the setting: a palatial estate, servants standing by, lush landscaping, plush furnishing, trickling fountains, the finest food and wine, the glorious king, the beautiful Queen, and befuddled Haman.

And now the Offer just hangs in the air, for the third time. What's a young follower of Christ to do?

Back when I was twenty, I received an offer. A pastor named Vern called my home. I was dressed for work—ready to stack apples and bundle scallions as a produce clerk. I was just about to leave, when Vern called with an offer. He said, "Bill, how would you like to quit your job at the grocery store, and come and work with me at my church, and become our children's pastor?"

For me, it was a dream come true. I had known since age eight that God wanted me to be a pastor, but I had balked at actually taking steps in that direction. Part of me loved the idea; another part of me hated the idea. Then God, through Vern, gave an offer I couldn't refuse.

I asked him to tell me about the job. He did. It seemed like a great fit.

I asked, "How much?"

He said, "One hundred ten dollars a week." Minimum wage exactly.

I said "Hired."

That's how I got my start in full-time vocational ministry. Someone else made an offer—we'll let that represent grace. I accepted the offer—we'll let that represent faith.

I'm not a dancer—I grew up fundamentalist so I never acquired rhythm—but life with God is a grace/faith two-step. He offers grace. We accept the offer through faith. When anything good happens in or because of our lives, grace is the principal cause and faith is the instrumental cause. It's as if grace is the life-giving water stored in a tank and faith is the pipeline that delivers it. We are saved *by* grace *through* faith (Ephesians 2:8). And we keep on going with that simple pairing till we suck in our last molecule of earthly oxygen and wake up in the land of endless sunshine.

Esther and her people are about to be saved by grace through faith. All that remains is for her to take hold of the Offer.

What Does Faith Look Like?

Faith is a situation-specific shape-shifter. If I tell my six-year old son to sit still and I'll bring him some birthday cake, faith looks like a boy sitting still, though wiggling with anticipation. If I tell him to run upstairs because there's a new Iron Man robot in his bedroom, faith means jumping out of his chair and running up the stairs. Faith is situation-specific.

So, depending on the situation, and depending on the precise command from God for the moment, faith's expression can take *opposite* forms. Here are some examples:

INACTION. When the Jews were pinned against the Red Sea with Pharaoh's army in hot pursuit, what did Moses say? "Just stand where you are and watch the LORD rescue you..."

(Exodus 14:13). Sometimes faith requires that you stand still and do nothing even as everything inside you screams to act.

But other times, faith looks like just the opposite.

ACTION. Jesus walked on water, blowing some gaskets in his disciples' brains in the process. But irrepressible Peter had enough faith for the lot of them. He asked Jesus to command him to step out of the boat and walk on water too. Jesus was happy to comply, and Peter went over the side of the boat and walked on water (Matthew 14:28, 29). Peter took action and earned a spot in faith's Hall of Fame.

WAITING. Before God knocked over the walls of Jericho, he commanded Israel to march around the city once a day for six straight days. In silence. You can imagine the generals arguing with Joshua to attack and get this war over. But God had a plan, and in his plan, faith meant postponing the attack until the seventh day (Joshua 6:1-21). Sometimes waiting makes you a champion of faith.

QUIT WAITING. The prophet Elijah had just given the priests of the false god Baal a newsworthy whack upside their idol-worshipping heads. Then he turned to the Jews who had been waffling between Baal and the true God of Israel, and issued an ultimatum. "How long are you going to waver between two opinions? If the Lord is God, follow him! But if Baal is God, then follow him!" (1 Kings 18:21). Make up your mind, quit waiting, act right now. The time for waiting was over.

ASK. Jesus taught his followers to persist in prayer. "Keep on asking," he said, "and you will be given what you ask for" (Matthew 7:7). Sometimes faith means persevering in prayer.

DON'T ASK. Other times, persevering would be a sign that you don't trust God. The apostle Paul suffered a mysterious ailment that he called his "thorn in the flesh." He prayed that

God would remove it. Then prayed again. And then he prayed again. After the third time, God told him to change his tune. Paul's thorn in the flesh would be a permanent reminder that with God's grace in his life, he had all he needed (2 Corinthians 12:8, 9). His continued prayer to remove it would be a sign of unbelief.

Act, don't act, wait, quit waiting, ask, don't ask. Faith is a situation-specific shape-shifter. This makes life with God a never-boring, soul-stretching, unpredictable adventure.

Faith is Like Pasta Sauce

My Grandpa, an Italian from the old country, taught my mom, who is not Italian, how to make mouth-watering pasta sauce. My mom taught me. But she did it over the telephone, from over 1,200 miles away. I lived in Chicago. My parents had moved to Florida. One day, I got a taste for Mom's pasta sauce, and called for the recipe.

She couldn't give it to me. I don't mean she wouldn't, she couldn't. She rattled off some ingredients: start with some good tomato sauce, and some paste, add a little oregano, some basil, some red wine. She asked what else I had in the fridge and the cupboard to throw into the mix.

"Whoa!" I interrupted her. "I need to know exactly how much tomato sauce and how much red wine and how many teaspoons of spice and exactly how many garlic cloves." She laughed. "I don't know, honey. You just do it by feel."

I wanted precision. She offered approximations.

I wanted a replicable recipe. She offered seat-of-the-pants creativity.

I cooked by works. She cooked by faith.

Her way was better.

By revealing faith as a situation-specific shape-shifter, Scripture has cornered us into a dynamic, seat-of-the-pants, imprecise, messy-but-delicious relationship with the Living God. This way is better. No cookie-cutters. No replicable recipes. No Christian clones. It's a dance, and no two children of God have the same moves.

And in case you scratch your head wondering how you can ever decide what faith should look like in your situation, it's simple. Just do the opposite of what your self-protective instincts tell you and you'll probably be okay. Because, though faith may take a myriad of outward forms, faith's inner reality stays the same: *faith always involves risking your neck on the character and promises of God.*

It takes no faith at all to preserve your status quo.

Plus, even if you choose wrong, you can't go wrong, because God rewards faith and all who seek him by it, even if we selected the wrong option, but did so faithfully.

Make this your mantra: *my job is faith; God's job is outcomes.*

Faith can't lose.

Now, it's Esther's turn. She can either slink back to her self-protective lifelessness or risk the life she has to gain the life she wants. The Offer is dangling there for the third time. Time to put up or shut up. Time for faith—the risky kind that reveals her identity as a Jew, thus making her immediately vulnerable in ways she has not known before.

What happens?

And so Queen Esther replied, "If Your Majesty is pleased with me and wants to grant my request, my petition is that my life and the lives of my people will be spared. For my people and I have been sold to those who would kill, slaughter, and annihilate us. If we had only been sold as slaves, I could remain quiet, for that would have been a matter too trivial to warrant disturbing the king." (Esther 7:3, 4)

In a history-making, world-class, age-defining, genocide-averting moment of faith, she goes for Haman's jugular. You have to risk the life you have to gain the life you want. If you must take a risk that could result in your death, make sure you follow Esther's three-part paradigm:

The Three Part Paradigm

First, find a transpersonal purpose.

If you're going to turn everything upside down and risk it all, make sure you risk it for something bigger than yourself. A ritzier car, a trendier neighborhood, a trophy wife, and mortgaging yourself to your eyeballs to buy a massive house do not constitute a transpersonal purpose. Some of those things might be okay, but that's not why God created you. God created you to go beyond yourself and to contribute to his transcendent cause. Esther petitions not only for her own life, but also for the lives of her people. Faith seeks a cause worth living for and dying for.

Second, use a tactical approach.

Esther discerns the king's self-absorption as well as his fragile ego. So she appeals to both his self-interest and his bottom line. She crafts her words to elicit the best possible response from the king. Jesus counsels us to be "wise as serpents" (Matthew 10:16). Esther runs a clinic.

Third, practice direct engagement.

Go straight at the craziness. Esther doesn't wimp out: "Well, I'm sure it's all a big mistake, Haman, and I know you really didn't mean it, and years from now we'll all laugh about this..."

No.

She doesn't back down from the real issue; she states it cleanly and directly. In the never-ending battle of good vs. evil somebody has to call evil "evil" to Evil's face.

Don't Stop Short

The king and Haman sit dazed and confused. What is she talking about? The slack jawed King speaks: "Who would do such a thing?' King Xerxes demanded. 'Who would dare touch you'" (Esther 7:5)?

In 1660 authorities gave a preacher named John Bunyan a choice: quit preaching without a license, or go to jail. Bunyan had converted to a new sect, called the Baptists, and was conducting services in rural villages around Bedford. Local officials found him to be in violation of the Conventicle Act, which permitted public preaching to ordained Church of England clergy only.

Bunyan made a life-changing decision: "If you release me from prison today, I shall resume preaching tomorrow," he told them.

He remained in prison twelve years.

How far will you stick your neck out for what you believe? Would you sacrifice money, friends, or status to gain the life God designed you for? Would you give up, "houses or brothers or sisters or father or mother or children or property," for Jesus' sake, if it meant an abundant life here, and a super-abundant life hereafter (Matthew 19:29)?

Esther has struck the first blow against Haman, and now it was time to go in for the kill. But is it worth it? Once she names him, she can never turn back. This is a point of no return. Everything is at stake. She lives in the same palace where Haman works. He has the king's support. She knows what a Son of Belial he is, and she has played nice. She says "Good morning" when he passes in the hallway. She smiles at him during social functions.

She has coped with world-class OPC, but now it's "go time." The king has asked who would dare lay a hand on her. Will Esther stop short? Or will her faith carry her all the way?

> Esther replied, "This wicked Haman is our enemy." Haman grew pale with fright before the king and queen. Then the king jumped to his feet in a rage and went out into the palace garden. But Haman stayed behind to plead for his life with Queen Esther, for he knew that he was doomed. In despair he fell on the couch where Queen Esther was reclining, just as the king returned from the palace garden. "Will he even assault the queen right here in the palace, before my very eyes?" the king roared. And as soon as the king spoke, his attendants covered Haman's face, signaling his doom. Then Harbona, one of the king's eunuchs, said, "Haman has set up a gallows that stands seventy-five feet tall in his own courtyard. He intended to use it to hang Mordecai, the man who saved the king from assassination." "Then hang Haman on it!" the king ordered." (Esther 7:6-9)

When you hear the words, "church picnic," the last thought that crosses your mind is a group of drunk, tattooed, unshaven motorcycle dudes terrorizing happy, picnicking Christians. I know it was the last thing I expected.

Make that next to last. The last thing any of us expected was that a petite woman in our singles group would rescue us.

Our church singles group planned a picnic in the forest preserves north of Chicago. We were minding our own business, tossing around a football, and grilling Italian sausages and burgers, when the "visitors" came. A group of bikers a hundred yards away decided that beer wasn't filling enough. So they joined our picnic, uninvited. The biggest biker wore a leather vest over bare skin. His hairy chest only accentuated his big biceps and his bigger gut. He walked into our pavilion and picked up a whole watermelon, an unopened back of chips, and then the large knife he would need to slice the watermelon. We stood stupefied as he sauntered back to his laughing buddies.

As a young man, I felt ashamed. I knew he'd knock me over with one swipe. The rest of the guys felt the same. As our dispirited bachelor herd huddled under our picnic pavilion, we wrung our wimpy hands, wondering what to do.

That's when Diana came back from the football game. "What did that guy want?" she asked. Diana was a small woman with blonde hair that reached her waist. She had been part of our singles group for about a year; a fun, spunky, dedicated Christian.

"He stole our watermelon," we whined. "And our potato chips!"

I look back in unmixed embarrassment over my colossal chicken-hood. Evil stared us—me—in the face, and I looked away. I stopped short of confronting OPC. "Uh... didn't Jesus say, 'Blessed are the peacemakers?' Yeah, that's it, we're peacemakers. And who needs watermelon, anyway?"

Evidently, Diana did. We poured forth our cringe-worthy story, and watched her indignation mount. "That's not right. I'm getting our stuff back." We then watched, thunderstruck, as five-foot-four, petite Diana marched into the midst of the biker beer-party, got in the big biker's face, and—hands on hips—demanded our watermelon, chips, and knife back.

I think Esther and Diana shared some spiritual DNA. When the time came for Esther to pull the trigger, she stuck her finger in Haman's scrawny chest and announced, "This wicked Haman is our enemy." Evil is evil, and somebody's got to say it, and damn the consequences.

We listened in awe as Diana preached, "We're Christians. And we follow Jesus. And what you did is wrong. You need Jesus in your life. Is this the kind of life you really want to live? Getting drunk and bullying people around?"

I'm still in awe as I think of it. The poor biker-dude must have felt that awe too, because he looked down at Diana and blushed redder than his beer could account for. He apologized—"Uh, wow, I'm sorry. I didn't know you guys were a church"—and returned our watermelon and knife. It was too late for the chips.

Faith is the victory. And Diana, well she's royalty.

Even if Diana hadn't gotten our watermelon back, I know God was pleased with her risk-taking faith. And even if King Xerxes had backed Haman, this moment goes down in history as a world-class triumph of audacious faith.

Notice the King's first reaction: he gets up and walks out.

Passive Craziness

Let's call this passive craziness, characterized by four sissy-defining qualities:

1. *Emotional Over-reaction.* Verse 7 says Xerxes hit the roof. Beware of a wimp who's pushed too far. He'll hit the roof. Insecurity breeds drama and drama thrives on crisis.

2. *Exit strategy.* Without a word, Xerxes escapes to the palace gardens. OPC, the passive variety, comes in endless forms. Some might take a pounding and hang their head, or justify it, or pretend it's okay. Still others deny it, or crack jokes, or numb out with drugs and drink and sex and porn. In any case, the king represents an inner devotion to do whatever it takes to avoid conflict, turmoil, and emotion—and to keep life as comfy as possible. Meet your Inner Wimp.

3. *Unfair fighting.* Was Haman really trying to assault the Queen? No. He just fell on the couch. So what does the king execute him for? For assaulting the Queen—the one crime that he wasn't guilty of. Even more irony!

4. *Mental laziness.* For about the fiftieth time, the king doesn't know what to do, and in steps a—wait for it—eunuch. How can you read this and not laugh? Mr. Eunuch, at this point the manliest man in the room, points out the window to the handy dandy gallows that Haman had so conveniently built just last night. For Mordecai. And the eunuch steps forward to say, "Excuse me, King. But there's an excellent gallows out there, that Haman just finished... Perhaps... well, you decide." He adds the tidbit, that "the gallows was built for Mordecai, who just so happened to be the King's special lifesaver, don't forget."

That eunuch had bigger... uhhh... well... "guts" than the other two men in the room.

Passive craziness comes with its own set of dangers. Watch out.

Dangerous Craziness

And then there's wretched old Haman. He's got the dangerous craziness. Bully craziness. Sadist craziness. Let's note four qualities.

1. *Vulnerable targets.* For him it was the Jews. For you it might be your kids, your wife, the elderly, your employees, the one who makes mistakes. The one all the cool kids call ugly. Dangerous OPC can sniff out vulnerabilities from a mile away and exploit it in a million ways.

2. *Fear motivation,* v. 6. Fear is the underlying emotion for most bullies. And the thing they fear the most is discovering their own incompetence. But so what? Esther goes in for the kill anyway.

3. *Boundary violation,* v. 8. He gets way too close to Esther, and gets spiked to death for it. Haman violated Esther's physical boundaries. Bullies have very little sense of their own selves. They don't get the concept of boundaries. Emotional boundaries. Physical boundaries. Financial boundaries. If there's a legitimate boundary, a person with Dangerous OPC will cross it. And once they cross one boundary with impunity, the sky's the limit. Watch out.

4. *Self-destruction.* Haman was hung on his own gallows. OPC always boomerangs. The dirt you dish gets dished back to you. Be careful what ingredients you throw into the stew of how you treat other people, because one day you'll have to sit down and eat it.

> The wicked conceive evil; they are pregnant with trouble and give birth to lies. They dig a pit to trap others and then fall into it themselves. They make trouble, but it backfires on them. They plan violence for others, but it falls on their own heads. (Psalm 7:14-16)

So they hanged Haman on the gallows he had set up for Mordecai, and the king's anger was pacified. (Esther 7:10)

You can't shy away from a necessary fight. You can't let OPC destroy your life or make victims out of others. Sooner or later, somebody has to stick her neck out and change the equation of power.

King Solomon wrote:

There is a time for everything, a season for every activity under heaven. A time to be born and a time to die. A time to plant and a time to harvest. A time to kill and a time to heal. A time to tear down and a time to rebuild. A time to cry and a time to laugh. A time to grieve and a time to dance. A time to scatter stones and a time to gather stones. A time to embrace and a time to turn away. A time to search and a time to lose. A time to keep and a time to throw away. A time to tear and a time to mend. A time to be quiet and a time to speak up. A time to love and a time to hate. A time for war and a time for peace. (Ecclesiastes 3:1-8)

A time to kill, a time to hate, a time of war, a time to die. A time to not be nice. But a time to go in for the kill. That's godly. That's righteous. That's faith in action. That's Esther.

Hopefully that's you and that's me.

Let's go get our watermelon back.

𒀭𒍣𒊩𒐊𒐊𒐊⸱𒐊

Reflections

Reflections 1: God takes it personally when anybody messes with you; he's already plotting revenge on the OPC in your life.

He's already involved even when it doesn't look like it. So far, we have read seven chapters in this book, and do you know who has not even been mentioned once: God!

Why not? God is not mentioned in Esther, because so many times that's the way life with him feels—it feels as if God is absent, or silent, or distant. How many times have you felt like this?

But God passionately opposes OPC. He hates it. He's ultra active whenever it happens. He's working. Even when you're fretting, and giving yourself an ulcer, God knows. He sees evil for what it is.

God takes it personally when anybody messes with his children.

And he is working and planning and preparing to solve the problem of Other People's Craziness in your life.

But you wonder what's taking him so long.

Sometimes, he's waiting for faith, even if it's baby steps. You have to be willing to fight the fight of faith.

> For the eyes of the LORD run to and fro throughout the whole earth, to show Himself strong on behalf of those whose heart is loyal to Him. (2 Chronicles 16:9, NKJV)

Sometimes, you have to just stop putting out the welcome mat for Other People's Craziness. That bold faith, in a sense, triggers God's action.

But you worry. You think, *What if I take a step of faith, and God lets me down? I have to solve my problems myself. I have to take matters into my own hands. God doesn't really see my faith.*

Even that thinking is a kind of faith. It's an inverse faith in an inverse god. The truth is opposite.

Grace is obligated to faith.

Wherever God sees a speck of faith, he is pleased. He scrambles his angelic fighter pilots, and sends down an absolutely perfect, all-sufficient, abundant, shockingly appropriate supply of grace.

If you live a life of faith, God is obligated to show you an experience of grace—of blessing and riches that money can't buy.

Scripture teaches, and theology observes, that God is free. This means that God is under no compulsion to bless anybody. God is nobody's debtor; God does not have to do anything for anybody.

There are no constraints on God—except for this: God is constrained by his own character and Word. God cannot be other than what he is. And that means that when God makes a promise, then God not only will, but must, fulfill that promise.

Reflections 2: God has promised to honor faith wherever he sees it.

Grace is obligated to faith, and to faith alone. Grace is not obligated to performance; and grace is not obligated to success stories.

Grace is obligated to a young woman [Esther] who is in a crazy, dangerous mess way over her head—just because she took a step of faith into a solution that grace had already pre-packaged and supplied.

I'm not writing to tell you to be a better person. Or to be a more moral person, or a more decent person. I think the very fact you're reading this already says you want to be a better person.

I'm writing to urge you to be a more FAITH-FILLED person, who trusts day by day and moment by moment in God's character and Word, letting Christ-in-you shine, and believing he is ready to make you into the person you've always wanted to be.

Faith is the victory, no matter how the cookie crumbles.

Can God bring down your enemies? Can he humble those who would humiliate you? Can he solve your financial problems? Can he provide for you in your golden years? Can he overcome your addictions? Can he erase your guilt and shame? Can he help you love your spouse? Your ex-? Can he help you forgive the person who wounded you? Will he punish the ungodly? Will he execute vengeance in his own time, in his own way?

Can God bring down the Hamans in your life without your help?

Trust him. Believe him enough to act like he is true. "And this is the victory that has overcome the world—our faith" (1 John 5:4, NKJV).

Reflections 3: Leave room for God as you deal with OPC.

Jesus lives in you so that your life can be a recap of his, only with your personality and dreams brought to their highest fulfillment.

Every phase of your Christian life rests on God's grace

Christ gave his life for you and, when you receive him, he puts his life in you that he might live his life through you. So the Bible says,

> I have been crucified with Christ; it is no longer I who live, but Christ lives in me; and the life which I now live in the flesh I live by faith in the Son of God, who loved me and gave Himself for me. (Galatians 2:20, NKJV)

By definition, every child of God enjoys the permanent indwelling of the Lord Jesus Christ.

Like many Christians, however, you might worry that Jesus will suck out your personality and turn you into a mindless drone. You can relax; he doesn't erase you when he lives through you. He actually makes you more yourself than you could ever be without him.

Jesus came to make you You, with all the color added.

Reflections 4: The power is activated by faith, no matter how you feel.

It's at this point that so many of us experience a major paradox: if Christ is living in me, why am I still such a mess? If he's working his grace through me, he's not doing a very good job of it. How do I make this whole system work? What will it take for my life to display the power of the living Christ?

It's simple, though not always easy.

The power of Jesus is activated by faith. "The life which I now live in the flesh I live by faith in the Son of God..." (Galatians 2:20, NKJV).

All those self-help books that people line up to buy work for a while, but so many times the help is temporary. There are rarely easy, fast fixes to the problems of our lives. Growth in grace takes time. It takes deep faith shining forth in determination and grit. It takes a good, long look into the face—the names and characteristics—of God. It takes time spent with Jesus in God's Word. Self-help is one thing, and it's fine. But nurturing a growing confidence in God and his grace—that's where the lasting magic is.

Think about the story and its progress here in Esther. The people are doomed. Esther is doomed. She carries a growing burden to save her people. It is her task, her role, her responsibility. And that is exactly how God begins to deal with us. We feel the pressure of our problems, of OPC, and of our disconnection with God, like a heavy burden slumping our shoulders and sagging our backs.

Then, just when we can't bear it one second longer, God shoves us out of the story altogether and takes care of business without the tiniest bit of help from us. That's grace. God moves in. He bears the burden. He accomplishes the task. He takes responsibility. He saves the day. Thank God for the Cross of Christ. Thank God for those incredible words, "It is finished!" (John 19:30).

God does it all. Salvation and every blessing post-salvation in our lives are his work, his effort, his power, and his grace.

So what do we do? We step into what God has already done and ask to partake of the benefits. That's called faith. Esther will take that leap of faith in the very next chapter.

Therefore, the central battle that you have to fight every single day is the battle of faith—the battle to keep on trusting God. To keep on believing that the power of Jesus will work in you, when you face a nasty ex-, or a crazy neighbor, or a cruel boss, or a passive child.

If your mind defines Christianity as YOU following Jesus, or as YOU doing good works, or as YOU becoming a moral scout, or as YOU being the moral police of our society, you will fail. You'll wear out. You'll fall. Because you will demote the majestic plan of an omnipotent God to menial set of meaningless chores accomplished by the sweat of your brow, and that view is fatal.

It is God's work. Faith is the gutsy determination to keep on trusting him in every trial, in every tough time, and in every circumstance when OPC threatens you.

Oh how we long for the easy button, the magic pill, the healing mantra! Easy. Fast. Done.

In truth, if we really stop and reflect, we know in our hearts that the authentic way of unseating the Hamans in this life is a day by day, hour by hour, minute by minute adventure of faith. It's faith that wins our battles. Faith in family, friends, doctors, planners—yes. But ultimately faith in God.

When you wrestle yourself to a place of faith in God and his Word, every other victory will fall into place.

Faith always prevails with God.

FOR REFLECTION AND DISCUSSION: Has faith ever taken opposite forms in your life? How? Describe a time when faith meant making two opposite choices. What do you think of the comparison between faith and pasta sauce? Does that free you or frustrate you? Describe a time when you got caught up looking for feelings from God. How might you do things differently if you could go back?

CHAPTER 11

Fighting Back, Holy-Style

ALL OF A SUDDEN, THE TABLES HAVE turned. With a seven-story drop, Haman's head, with its beady little eyes, probably got ripped off like a bowling ball, and will roll down the gutter of history for time and eternity. And the only reason you might think that's a horrible thing to say is because you were never in his crosshairs. To this day, Jews still cheer Haman's death.

> On that same day King Xerxes gave the estate of Haman, the enemy of the Jews, to Queen Esther. Then Mordecai was brought before the king, for Esther had told the king how they were related. The king took off his signet ring—which he had taken back from Haman—and gave it to Mordecai. And Esther appointed Mordecai to be in charge of Haman's property. (Esther 8:1, 2)

What's going on here? We're watching Esther and Mordecai shake free from Other People's Craziness once for all. Done with the mindgames. Victors over the insanity.

The two greatest sources of OPC in their lives are 1) Haman, and 2) the king.

Haman's corpse hangs outside, down about a block, and to the left. He's been impaled in his own back yard. At the top of a seven-story gallows. Dangling, dead, and limp for all the world to see.

No more craziness from that guy. I'm not advocating that you handle OPC this way, but it worked nicely for Esther.

The king has handed over the ring of authority and power to Mordecai. All this stress makes the king very, very sleepy. He needs cookies and a nice nap. So he just vanishes himself.

Again.

The two great sources of OPC have both been nullified. How?

By grace through faith. Let us recap. Remember, grace is what God does for us, through us, and on our behalf.

- God put Esther on the queenly throne of Persia. So she was pre-positioned before Haman passed his murderous decree. Grace.
- God empowered Esther to come before the king. Grace.
- God made Esther "find favor [grace] in the sight of the king." Grace.
- God made it so the king dangled a breathtaking offer before Esther: "ask for whatever you want, and I will give it to you, up to half the kingdom." All she had to do was ASK. Grace.
- God turned the tables on Haman, so that Haman started his free-fall without anybody's help—without even any faith—on the part of Esther or anybody else. God did it. Grace.
- God has so designed the world, that evil is its own worst enemy. He did not design evil. He did not create it. God is not in any way the author of evil (James 1:13,

Habakkuk 2:13). The devil, demons, and humans did that.

But God sprung a trap. He made evil eat evil, like a snake eating its own tail.

When OPC meets OPC, it's like matter meeting anti-matter. Something's going to blow. OPC-Haman-style walked himself to the end of the plank, and OPC-King-style shoved him off. Evil is its own worst enemy.

Brilliant turnabout, God. Amazing grace.

Grace is what only God can do.

Faith, on the other hand, is what you must do. And remember, that faith can take a multitude of forms.

- Esther fasted and prayed; she invited the rest of the Jews to fast and pray, too. Faith.
- Esther took the bold risk of a surprise appearance before King Xerxes—which was potentially punishable by death. Faith.
- Esther only had to ask, and the king would give it to her, up to half the kingdom. Faith.
- Esther asked the king and Haman to come to her party. She didn't know how she was going to plead for her people's life, but, by issuing the invitation, she crossed the point of no return. Faith.
- When the time came, Esther asked the king to save her life and her people's life. And she stopped beating around the bush, and took her leap of... Faith.

What I'm saying is simple. The way God knocks out the OPC in your life is by the one-two punch of Grace and Faith.

Which makes me ask myself, and you with me, what step of faith could I take that would knock out a big chunk of OPC in my life right now? I'm not asking us to *make* something happen. That's God's job. I'm asking us to step into that which God can make happen. There's a difference.

What step of faith will crush some of the OPC in your life?

Ask, and become just like Esther.

The Real Me

Now once more Esther came before the king, falling down at his feet and begging him with tears to stop Haman's evil plot against the Jews. Again the king held out the gold scepter to Esther. So she rose and stood before him and said, "If Your Majesty is pleased with me and if he thinks it is right, send out a decree reversing Haman's orders to destroy the Jews throughout all the provinces of the king. For how can I endure to see my people and my family slaughtered and destroyed?" (Esther 8:3-6)

There are two really important developments here for OPC management in your life.

The first one strikes at the heart of OPC. For the first time in the book of Esther, Esther is comfortable in her own skin. She is a woman. She is a Jew. She is Mordecai's cousin. She is queen. She is who she is, and finally, she's not hiding any of it.

Her Oscar-worthy performance is over. She can exit the virtual world and engage the real one.

OPC always puts its crosshairs on your IDENTITY. The real you. OPC attempts to make you into something other than what you really are. People want to crush you, limit you, label you, define you. And they will, if you let them.

The biggest temptation Esther has faced in this whole story is the temptation to hide her true self.

Her Jewishness.

Her womanliness.

Her royalty.

Finally, she owns all of it. No more hiding. No more pretending to be something she wasn't. *Here I am. Love me. Hate me. Accept me. Kill me. I'm not playing your crazy game anymore. This is the real me.*

Full acknowledgment of her identity. That's the first development.

The Royal We

The second one is her total commitment to her people. "How can I endure to see my people and my family slaughtered and destroyed?"

She's no longer in isolation. She's in community. Not only am I a Jew, singularly, I belong to the family of the Jews, collectively. What happens to them happens to me.

She's not worried about just her own skin anymore. Now, it's pedal to the metal for her people, and hopefully the quirky king won't get sick of her and chop off her head.

Jesus said, "I will build my church" (Matthew 16:18).

Paul said, "And the eye cannot say to the hand, 'I have no need of you'; nor again the head to the feet, 'I have no need of you'" (1 Corinthians 12:21, NKJV).

Esther leaped two great hurdles in rising above OPC: she found her true identity and she found her true community.

OPC will wreck both if you let it.

The Ring of Power

Then King Xerxes said to Queen Esther and Mordecai the Jew, "I have given Esther the estate of Haman, and he has been hanged on the gallows because he tried to destroy the Jews. Now go ahead and send a message to the Jews in the king's name, telling them whatever you want, and seal it with the king's signet ring. But remember that whatever is written in the king's name and sealed with his ring can never be revoked." (Esther 8:7, 8)

A lot of cars have tracking systems installed, so if the car gets stolen, the police can find it.

Let's put a tracking device on the SIGNET RING. This is the ring of power. Whoever has possession of the ring has all the king's power. That person can make laws, spend money, and sign decrees. That person possesses power of life and death.

So let's track the ring throughout Esther's story.

Stage One: The King. The king starts out with the ring. But think of all the craziness when the ring of power is in the hands of a passive ruler who rarely makes decisions and generally waits for other people to do his thinking for him.

Stage Two: Haman. So, in chapter three, the king transfers the ring of power to Haman (3:10). Haman immediately drafts the law to slaughter the Jews and seals it with the ring of power. So the power has shifted from a passive wimpy ruler who can't make a decision, to an aggressive, hateful, dangerous ruler who cheapens human life and degrades people to satisfy his own narcissistic desires

Let me ask you something: right now, who's got the ring in your life? Who's really running your life?

Don't answer right away, because it's a complicated answer. You might say, "I am. I'm running my life."

The problem is that YOU are a collection of parts—
"members," the Bible calls them. For example:

> And do not present your members as instruments of
> unrighteousness to sin, but present yourselves to God as
> being alive from the dead, and your members as instruments
> of righteousness to God. (Romans 6:13, NKJV)

And so when you say, I'm running my life, I want to get
more specific.

Which *part* of you is running your life? Which member?

Is it your passive, wimpy side that is waiting for life to
happen, and fails to launch?

Is it your mean, critical, demeaning side that's constantly
sending out porcupine quills, and wounding everybody who
comes close?

Who's got the ring? Your Inner Haman or your Inner
King? Or your Inner Brat, Inner Thug, Inner Victim, Inner
Whiner, Inner Pharisee, Inner Fraud, Inner Wimp, Inner
Bully, Inner Pervert? Which member at your internal
committee table is really calling the shots?

Breathe.

Stage Three: Back to the King. From chapter three to
chapter seven, Haman clutches the ring of power in his bony
little fingers. And now, on the way to the gallows to spike
Haman, the king steps in. He speaks to the eunuchs who are
leading Haman away and says, "Wait a minute, uh, fellas."
They stop. The king reaches over, grabs Haman's hand.

I wonder what Haman was thinking and saying and doing.
Was he screaming? Was he crying? Yelling? Cursing? What's
he doing?

Imagine the moment of hope when the king grabs his
hand. *Oh joy,* thinks Haman. *The King is going to make nice.
Thank you, dearest idol Ashtarte, thank you.*

The king says, "Haman, one more thing before you go—I need my ring back. Thanks so much. Good luck. Cheerio. Okay, er, men. Carry on."

So our ring-of-power tracking system has followed the ring from the king to Haman and back to the king (8:2).

Stage Four: Mordecai. But since His Highness has a dependent, wimpy streak, he can't handle the ring. So, he looks at Mordecai. 'You look like a ringy sort of fellow. Want this?" Just like that, the king tosses the ring of power to him.

From the king, to Haman, to the king, to Mordecai.

It's a ring in motion.

Just like it is in our lives today.

Who has the ring of power in your life, right now? Either you surrender the ring to the crazies, or deliver it to the Mordecai-Esther team within, representing you at your very best. You living by faith. You under the influence of God, the Holy Spirit, and Jesus. You listening to the voice of God in his Word. You going deep and mature in Scripture. You sane, and whole and happy in Jesus.

Who's holding the ring of power? Some nut lurking in your inner Animal Farm? Or your noble spirit—the part of you that responds to God? Who's got the ring?

Esther's lesson is beautiful. You have the power to kick the crazies out of the driver's seat of your inner world. You have the power to put the real you—the "you" who fully owns your identity and royalty and dominion, and the "you" who is wholesomely connected to community—in the driver's seat, and to buckle that "you" in for the long haul.

Thank God Mordecai finally holds that glorious ring of dominion.

And thank God when the noblest part of you lays hold of that same God-given power.

The Champion

So on June 25 the king's secretaries were summoned. As Mordecai dictated, they wrote a decree to the Jews and to the princes, governors, and local officials of all the 127 provinces stretching from India to Ethiopia. The decree was written in the scripts and languages of all the peoples of the empire, including the Jews. Mordecai wrote in the name of King Xerxes and sealed the message with the king's signet ring. He sent the letters by swift messengers, who rode horses especially bred for the king's service. The king's decree gave the Jews in every city authority to unite to defend their lives. They were allowed to kill, slaughter, and annihilate anyone of any nationality or province who might attack them or their children and wives, and to take the property of their enemies. The day chosen for this event throughout all the provinces of King Xerxes was March 7 of the next year. A copy of this decree was to be recognized as law in every province and proclaimed to all the people. That way the Jews would be ready on that day to take revenge on their enemies. So urged on by the king's command, the messengers rode out swiftly on horses bred for the king's service. The same decree was also issued at the fortress of Susa. (Esther 8:9-14)

If you choose life, you choose a fight.

OPC does not give up without a fight. The world, the flesh, and the devil are greedy little turf hounds, and must be evicted forcefully. You will not get your scepter back by accident. You will not regain your dominion by sitting passively by and wringing your hands. Not even changing your Facebook profile picture will do the trick. The battle is too fierce, and the stakes are much too high.

Thankfully, in this fight, you have a Champion. Jesus stands forever as the Champion you need in the fight for your life.

He fights for you. With you. Beside you. Within you. He's got your back. Jesus is slamming down adversaries in ways you can't begin to imagine. He's undercutting their power. He's thwarting their schemes. He's getting them to build their own metaphorical gallows, seventy feet tall (don't try this at home). He's tickling their stupidity neurons, making them bumbling fools, causing them one day soon to toss the stolen ring of power back your way.

That's my Jesus.

And he's your Jesus too, if you will have him.

You have a Champion.

But you might say, "If I have a champion, why do I feel so defeated?"

Faith IS the Victory

Because you still have to win the fight.

But what, exactly, is the fight?

Is it the fight to defeat your enemies? The fight to be a better person? The fight to be the most popular person with the most impressive posts on social media? The fight against your pet sins? The fight to lose weight, kill off bad habits, or practice better dental hygiene?

Not really.

We've already seen that the fight is a fight of faith. The fight to believe that what God has said is true, enough to act like it. That fight. Win that fight. Why? "And this is the victory that has overcome the world—our faith" (1 John 5:4, NKJV).

If you're looking for a truth that runs against most of the spiritual garbage out there, try this one on for size:

In the spiritual realm, victory isn't the victory; faith is the victory.

We Christians all too often celebrate the answered prayer, the miraculous healing, the successful risk-taker, the

177

victorious celebrity, the released hostage, and the overcoming sinner—while forgetting that God's power is most often shown in *weakness* (2 Corinthians 12:9).

Esther and Mordecai triumphed over Haman and the bumbling king. That's awesome.

But what about the thousands of cases where the story ends on a sad note? The prayer isn't answered. The illness isn't healed. The risky venture crashes and burns. The celebrity runs out of gigs. The true love never appears. The happily ever after vanishes in a misty haze.

Did OPC win the day?

Not necessarily.

When you've prayed three hundred times for your wayward child to come back to Christ, it's prayer #301 that rises above the fallen craziness of this world. Prayer when prayer makes no sense. Faith is the victory.

When you've trusted God for a good outcome 785 times, and still failed, it's act of trust #786 that stockpiles glorious rewards in eternity. Faith when faith makes no sense. Faith is the victory.

When you've given of your substance a thousand times to help those in need, or to worship God in your church, or to bless a hungry kid—when you've sown a thousand "seeds of faith"—and God still hasn't made you rich, it's sacrificial gift #1001 that garners riches money can't buy and rewards in heaven bankers can't repossess. Faith is the victory.

Your job is faith. God's job is outcomes.

And it's your faith—especially when faith makes no sense—that rises above OPC and restores your dominion, no matter who sits on the throne of your insanity-infested world.

The fight is a fight of faith.

Win the fight of faith, and all other victories fall into place—in God's [sometimes painfully slow] good time.

When you define victory as "intact faith in trying times," nobody can defeat you, nobody can dominate you, and nobody can overcome you. You are triumphant. You stand victorious in the battle of the ages.

People may scoff at you now. No one may know your name. But in the halls of heaven, you are a hero. And one day, you will step into an inheritance so glorious, it will take your celestial breath away.

Faith IS the victory, no matter how the chips may fall.

Mordecai drafted a law to fight back, and to slaughter anybody who dared to lift a finger against the Jews. And my concern is that most of the Christianized, wimp-i-fied church today thinks he was being too harsh, too unloving, and would relegate that kind of response to an Old Testament era when God was allegedly a God of wrath instead of love.

God has always been the same, in equally infinite measures of love and justice, mercy and wrath.

What we ought to do is cheer Mordecai. We ought to be glad that for the first time in eight long chapters the one who holds the ring of power actually has some guts.

And that the secret to having guts is not being a bully like Haman, or a weakling, like the king.

The secret is FAITH in God and his absolutely perfect, infinitely better than we can imagine, purposes.

Faith in a God who keeps his word, and sticks with you in trying circumstances and hides during the trial, just to prove to you you're stronger in grace than you realize.

Then Mordecai put on the royal robe of blue and white and the great crown of gold, and he wore an outer cloak of fine linen and purple. And the people of Susa celebrated the new decree. The Jews were filled with joy and gladness and were honored everywhere. In every city and province, wherever the king's decree arrived, the Jews rejoiced and had a great celebration and declared a public festival and holiday. And many of the people of the land became Jews themselves, for they feared what the Jews might do to them. (Esther 8:15-17)

Mordecai's robe was blue and white, and he had a gold turban—it wasn't a crown, but a turban.

That's like finally hanging the diplomas on the wall. In ancient Persia, only a king could wear blue and white, but Mordecai—who wasn't technically a king—believed in his own royalty, and wasn't afraid to say so.

He was a righteously dangerous, godly man.

The chapter ends on a note of joy, gladness, rejoicing, celebration, festival, and holiday. The dark cloud that hovered over God's people is gone.

OPC quivers in the corner, sucking its thumb, while grace and faith stand triumphant.

𒈦 𒀝 𒈨 𒐖 𒈦 𒐕

Reflections

Reflections 1: The first way to increase your faith is by digging deeply into the Bible, the Word of God.

Paul teaches, "So then faith comes by hearing, and hearing by the word of God" (Romans 10:17, NKJV). We need to stand on the deep things of God's Word. Not on emotion or sentimental memes, but on Scripture. Doctrine. Theology. The solid meat, not the milk.

Back in World War 2 days, author and Christian apologist Dorothy Sayers, wrote:

> It is a lie to say that doctrine does not matter; it matters enormously. It is fatal to let people suppose that Christianity is only a mode of feeling; it is vitally necessary to insist that it is first and foremost a rational explanation of the universe... [Christianity is] a hard, tough, exacting, and complex doctrine, steeped in a drastic and uncompromising realism. [9]

Because faith has to be IN something, and in this case, it is faith IN God and his Word. If you don't know God—his nature, and attributes and works and promises, his power and might, his holiness, his track record of absolute dependability, his beautiful dangerousness and grandeur and power—if you don't know God through his Word, your faith will be fragile. It will be occasional and weak.

But when you open the pages of Scripture and stare God in the face, profoundly and repeatedly, something happens to you. The Holy Spirit builds courage, muscle, and strength inside you. He constructs an indestructible edifice of faith. That's why Daniel declared, "[B]ut the people who know their God shall be strong, and carry out great exploits" (Daniel 11:32, NKJV). You can't trust a God you don't know, and you can't know him without sinking deep roots into the Bible.

So, instead of praying, "Lord, give me faith," try opening your Bible and digging in. Faith will grow as you come to know your glorious God, his invincible plan, and your all-sufficient identity in Christ.

Reflections 2: The second way to increase your faith is by passing the tests of adversity.

We could call this the accelerated method. James says, "[K]nowing that the testing of your faith produces endurance" (James 1:3, NAS95). You cannot let tough times make your faith evaporate. If you trust God in good times, that's nice, but so what? Anybody can do that. It's in the tough times—in crisis, in loss, in despair, in depression, in danger—that's when faith is proven and tested and tempered.

The giant pain machine called earth tests you all the time. It pushes you to your limit. You think you can't handle any more, but more comes anyway. What's going on?

> We are hard pressed on every side, yet not crushed; we are perplexed, but not in despair; persecuted, but not forsaken; struck down, but not destroyed—always carrying about in the body the dying of the Lord Jesus, that the life of Jesus also may be manifested in our body. (2 Corinthians 4:8-10, NKJV)

Hard pressed, yet not crushed.

Perplexed, but not in despair.

Persecuted, but not forsaken.

Struck down, but not destroyed.

Yes, the ugly snake of OPC rears its head against you over and over again. It strikes. It bites. It hurts.

But you've matured to a point where Other People's Craziness doesn't have the final say. It doesn't define you or own you. You've grown beyond it. You've risen above OPC. The mindgames might mess with you for a while, but over and over again, you overcome. Scripture loves to highlight the person of wisdom and maturity—the overcomer whose heart is full even in dire conditions, the battle-hardened sage who has tested and retested the all-sufficient grace of God, who declares, "My God is for me! Who can be against me?" (Romans 8:31).

You might have failed the same test over and over again. You might feel defeated. Stuck. Discouraged.

Do yourself a huge favor: rise above. Just once. Ask for God's help, and he'll give it. For one glorious moment, don't cave in. Don't indulge even one more pity party. Don't wimp out again. Take the risky step. Show the mature character. Fight for your life. Push back.

Just because you get shoved, it doesn't mean you have to fall over. God's grace is there for you in every situation. Believe. Trust. Rise above. Every test you pass builds muscle to pass future tests, which—until you're in heaven—will just keep coming.

FOR REFLECTION AND DISCUSSION: Do you use any kind of Bible reading plan? Are you part of a church? In what ways are you exposing yourself and your family to excellent instruction in the deep things of God and Scripture? What tests of life do you routinely fail? How might you grow into an overcomer?

CHAPTER 12

In Your Face, OPC!

THE MOST JOYFUL HOLIDAY OF JUDAISM is called the Feast of Purim. This holiday comes in February or March each year. It goes back two and a half millennia. All the way back to the Book of Esther.

To celebrate Purim, you need three things: Something relaxing to drink, a cookie with a fruit center, and a noisemaker. Go ahead and grab that stuff (or reasonable substitutes) before you read the rest of this chapter.

Other People's Craziness is running at epidemic levels right now. Crazies on your left, crazies on your right. Wimpy crazies. Dangerous crazies. Terrorist crazies. Religious crazies. Crazies in the grocery store, in the office at the next cubicle, in the church. A whole lot of them in the government. Dysfunctional people, utterly committed to sucking the life out of you.

Thankfully, as the book of Esther winds its way to a happy ending, we're given some advanced advice on rising above it all.

Blotting Out The Name

Once a year Jews read through the whole book of Esther, out loud. This is part of the ritual of the feast of Purim. As the book of Esther is read, whenever the people hear the name Haman, they "erase his name from the earth." They do this by making noise. They whistle, stomp their feet, shout, and blast their noisemakers. The idea is to blot out Haman's name.

I tried this at my church, a while back. We passed out noisemakers. As we read through these final chapters of Esther, and all throughout my sermon, whenever I said "Haman," pandemonium ensued.

It was fun. I even brought a decibel meter to determine which of our several services earned volume-bragging rights. It turned out to be the Classic service, which is mostly older people. I'm still not sure what that means.

Noble Power is Contagious

So on March 7 the two decrees of the king were put into effect. On that day, the enemies of the Jews had hoped to destroy them, but quite the opposite happened. The Jews gathered in their cities throughout all the king's provinces to defend themselves against anyone who might try to harm them. But no one could make a stand against them, for everyone was afraid of them. And all the commanders of the provinces, the princes, the governors, and the royal officials helped the Jews for fear of Mordecai. For Mordecai had been promoted in the king's palace, and his fame spread throughout all the provinces as he became more and more powerful. (Esther 9:1-4)

The balance of power has shifted. In the story's beginning, Other People's Craziness holds all the power. But by the end of the story, the power is in the hands of two truly noble souls.

And that power spreads throughout the whole land. Mordecai's growing position and power gives strength to all his people throughout the land.

Righteousness prevails.

One person standing up to evil, one person facing down a lifetime of OPC, one person can ignite a revolution in the nation, the church, the city, the family tree, the business, or the household.

Don't forget that it was God who, by his grace, opened the door for Esther and Mordecai to step into their true nobility.

He's done the same for you.

Step through that door.

Your playing nice might keep the peace, but it also keeps evil in power. Mordecai and Esther knew they were playing for keeps. They were all in.

And their faith inspired the nation, kicked a holocaust in the teeth, and saved countless lives.

Wouldn't you like that to be the story of your life? You might look in life's rearview mirror and see how crazy people have run your life in the past. Maybe they're running it today.

You may even feel stuck. *This is the way it is. This is how it has to be. This is how it's going to be until my cold, dead body rots in its grave.*

No!

Shed that lie, once for all.

You have the key to power. The door is opened.

You've always had it. Now take your stand, shake off the craziness, regain your dominion, and bless your world.

What comes next is a painfully difficult section of Scripture to read. The death and destruction described here are heartbreaking realities of earth's giant pain machine.

A Just War

But the Jews went ahead on the appointed day and struck down their enemies with the sword. They killed and annihilated their enemies and did as they pleased with those who hated them. They killed five hundred people in the fortress of Susa. They also killed Parshandatha, Dalphon, Aspatha, Poratha, Adalia, Aridatha, Parmashta, Arisai, Aridai, and Vaizatha—the ten sons of Haman son of Hammedatha, the enemy of the Jews. But they did not take any plunder. (Esther 9:5-10)

It's heartbreaking just to read it. What do we do with all this carnage?

Legendary evangelical philosopher, Arthur F. Holmes, aptly states, "To call war anything less than evil would be self-deception."[10] Holmes, noted for his long tenure at evangelical bastion, Wheaton College, wrote extensively on "Just War Theory." Drawing on both Judeo-Christian history, and Graeco-Roman philosophy, he concludes, "While it is true that the rule of law will neither cure nor wholly control a sin-ridden society, the fact remains that in God's creation all individual and societal activities are and should be rule-governed."

The same Savior who told his followers to "turn the other cheek" (Matthew 5:39), also told them, "[A]nd he who has no sword, let him sell his garment and buy one" (Luke 22:36, NKJV). Jesus was recognizing arguably the most self-evident truth in all of biblical theology: we live in a fallen world. A "sin-ridden society."

This fallen world is a morally corrupt pain machine.

Evil will come. We can't help it. The Bible admonishes us to not be surprised (John 16:33; 1 Peter 4:2). When that trouble turns violent, Scripture teaches that individuals have a right to defend themselves and their families, and governments have a right to declare war, according to certain limitations. Holmes and a wide variety of Christian theological positions find seven limitations on war within Scripture: A just cause (defense, not aggression), a just intention, the last resort (exhaust all other options), a formal declaration, limited objectives (peace, not pillage), proportionate means (just enough violence to win the peace), and non-combatant immunity.[11]

While we should not be judging ancient people by modern standards, it might be helpful to look at what happens in this chapter by the modern conclusions of Just War Theory.

Was there a "just cause?" Yes, the Jews were fighting in self-defense, attempting to avert a holocaust.

Was there a "just intention?" Yes, because they were not fighting to capture territory, to extend an empire, overthrow the government, or to steal wealth. They fought to subdue those who would destroy them.

Was this war "the last resort?" Yes, because all other options had been exhausted. The law passed by Mordecai gave them the legal right to fight back, and they did.

Was there a "formal declaration?" That's what Mordecai's law provided. It stipulated that if anyone attacked the Jews, the Jews would and could fight back.

Were there "limited objectives?" Yes, because it wasn't an overthrow or revolution. It was simply a displaced nation defending their lives, families, and possessions.

Were there "proportionate means?" Yes, with no weapons of mass destruction in sight. They used enough force to secure lasting peace and no more.

Was there "non-combatant immunity?" Yes, as the only people who were killed were those who went on the offensive against the Jews.

Even by modern standards, this ancient act of Jewish self-defense would pass muster as a Just War.

What are we to do with all this carnage?

We are to grieve. We are to be sad that Other People's Craziness rises to such destructive extremes. We should be righteously angry. We are to understand that life in this world is painfully hard, and that existence in the world to come, without Christ, is unspeakably heartbreaking. We are to leave all vengeance to God and government (Romans 13:1-6), and be prepared for the holy self-defense of our families and our lives.

And, we are to recognize that as long as we're stuck inside this giant pain machine called earth, we are to do all we can to make peace before war breaks out. This world is not our ultimate home, right? We are citizens of a heavenly kingdom. And we look forward every single day to that bright land where there is no war, and where the Prince of Peace rules from his glorious throne.

Securing the Peace

That evening, when the king was informed of the number of people killed in the fortress of Susa, he called for Queen Esther and said, "The Jews have killed five hundred people in the fortress of Susa alone and also Haman's ten sons. If they have done that here, what has happened in the rest of the provinces? But now, what more do you want? It will be granted to you; tell me and I will do it."

And Esther said, "If it please Your Majesty, give the Jews in Susa permission to do again tomorrow as they have done today, and have the bodies of Haman's ten sons hung from the gallows." So the king agreed, and the decree was announced in Susa. They also hung the bodies of Haman's ten sons from the gallows. Then the Jews at Susa gathered together on March 8 and killed three hundred more people, though again they took no plunder. Meanwhile, the other Jews throughout the king's provinces had gathered together to defend their lives. They gained relief from all their enemies, killing seventy-five thousand of those who hated them. But they did not take any plunder. (Esther 9:11-16)

War is hellish.

The Jews do what is necessary to secure lasting peace.

The devil has always harbored a special hatred of the Jews. They are God's "Chosen People." Even worse for Satan, they are the line of the Messiah—the Savior of the World, and, therefore, the Crusher of Satan's ugly little head.

What are the takeaways?

Accept that OPC is deadly serious business. While the Bible commands you to not take revenge, it does exhort you to contact authorities where the law has been broken, and let them—and God through them—take whatever revenge is needed (read Romans 13:1-6).

Support just wars.

Defend yourself and your family.

Never use violence, except as a necessary last resort to defend yourself.

And be extremely thankful for those noble warriors who have sacrificed themselves to gift you the freedoms you enjoy.

Throughout the provinces this was done on March 7. Then on the following day they rested, celebrating their victory with a day of feasting and gladness. But the Jews at Susa continued killing their enemies on the second day also, and then rested on the third day, making that their day of feasting and gladness.

So to this day, rural Jews living in unwalled villages celebrate an annual festival and holiday in late winter, when they rejoice and send gifts to each other. (Esther 9:17-19)

What was meant to be a holocaust became a military victory, sanctioned by law, and securing peace for years to come.

Other People's Craziness ranges from mildly silly to deadly serious. It's a broad-spectrum oppressor. When the Jews fought back, they fought back hard. They were fighting for their lives.

And so are you, in a sense. The stakes may not be literally life and death for you. I hope they're not (get help if they are). But in a metaphorical sense, your life is truly on the line.

Your truest life. Your deepest life, full of energy, adventure, and joy. God didn't create you to play the victim role. He didn't cast you as a passive weakling. He created the real you to shine like the brightest star in the night sky.

The ugly force called sin buries the true you in an avalanche of boredom, distractions, problems, debt, dysfunctions, disbelief, and despair. You might be tempted to give up. The story of your life might be one capitulation after another.

Your life—that precious spark of exuberant joy, ignited in childhood—may burn low.

So what are you going to do about it?

The little members of your internal committee wring their hands, and shake their heads. "Things will never change," they say. "Life is hard, so just make the best of it."

I pray somebody at that table—how about you—summons the guts to stand up and say, "Stop harassing me! This is my life, and I'm going to seize it!"

Because the nano-second you reach that conclusion, the powers of heaven mobilize on your behalf.

You Are Not Alone

God has geared up and stands with you. He's on your side in the fight for your life. You don't have to sell him on the idea. He's already sold.

The whole bulk of the Bible intends to communicate one singular reality: *God is better than you think he is, so that his heart is everlastingly inclined to be gracious to you.*

This is exactly the opposite of how most of us think and believe about God. Far too many people harbor the suspicion God can't wait to have them in his clutches, so he can suck every ounce of joy out of them.

But God is merciful, and gracious, and tenderhearted, and loving, and kind. He is gracious to you. His commitment to you outweighs your commitment to him a million-fold and beyond.

> He passed in front of Moses and said, "I am the LORD, I am the LORD, the merciful and gracious God. I am slow to anger and rich in unfailing love and faithfulness." (Exodus 34:6)

> But you, O Lord, are a merciful and gracious God, slow to get angry, full of unfailing love and truth. (Psalm 86:15)

> How kind the LORD is! How good he is! So merciful, this God of ours! (Psalm 116:5)

So when you face trials or craziness or loss or heartache or abuse, what do you think God is feeling? When you question your self-esteem. When you feel so uncertain. How does God look at you? Is he indifferent? Is he busy, off golfing? What is God feeling?

If you ever for a moment doubt the kindness and love of God toward you, look at Calvary. Look at the Cross, where Jesus died. And picture him—the only begotten Son of God, beloved, adored, cherished, precious—picture him hanging on the cross, absorbing your punishments and sins to set you free. To make you beautiful. To make you flawless. To make you perfect in God's eyes.

Do you want to see true love? Look at the Cross.

This is real love. It is not that we loved God, but that he loved us and sent his Son as a sacrifice to take away our sins. (1 John 4:10)

The flame of love you might feel for God on your very best day is hardly a flicker when seen against the fervent love of God for you even at your worst.

And if you think that before you can have God on your side, or before God will help you, that you have to improve, or be better, or lose twenty pounds, or fix up your life, you are mistaken.

The simple truth is you will never wait for God. He's ready to go. He's just waiting for you. Are you ready? Are you ready to conquer the OPC in your life? Do you want to shift the balance of power? Are you ready?

God is ready. He's been waiting for you. He's on your side. He sees OPC for what it is—an invasion on your dominion. He hates it. All heaven cheers you on.

Now, go take your life back.

A Holiday to Remember

Mordecai recorded these events and sent letters to the Jews near and far, throughout all the king's provinces, encouraging them to celebrate an annual festival on these two days. He told them to celebrate these days with feasting and gladness and by giving gifts to each other and to the poor. This would commemorate a time when the Jews gained relief from their enemies, when their sorrow was turned into gladness and their mourning into joy. So the Jews adopted Mordecai's suggestion and began this annual custom. Haman son of Hammedatha the Agagite, the enemy of the Jews, had plotted to crush and destroy them on the day and month determined by casting lots (the lots were called *purim*). But when Esther came before the king, he issued a decree causing Haman's evil plot to backfire, and Haman and his sons were hanged on the gallows. (That is why this celebration is called Purim, because it is the ancient word for casting lots.) So because of Mordecai's letter and because of what they had experienced, the Jews throughout the realm agreed to inaugurate this tradition and to pass it on to their descendants and to all who became Jews. They declared they would never fail to celebrate these two prescribed days at the appointed time each year. These days would be remembered and kept from generation to generation and celebrated by every family throughout the provinces and cities of the empire. These days would never cease to be celebrated among the Jews, nor would the memory of what happened ever die out among their descendants. Then Queen Esther, the daughter of Abihail, along with Mordecai the Jew, wrote another letter putting the queen's full authority behind Mordecai's letter to establish the Festival of Purim. In addition, letters wishing peace and security were sent to the Jews throughout the 127 provinces of the empire of Xerxes. These letters established the Festival of Purim—an annual celebration of these days at the appointed time, decreed by both Mordecai the Jew and Queen Esther. (The people decided to observe this festival, just as they had decided for themselves and their descendants to establish the times of fasting and mourning.) So the command of Esther confirmed the practices of Purim, and it was all written down in the records. (Esther 9:20-32)

God is into commemorating because we are into forgetting. This Feast of Purim continues, even today, as one of the most spectacular celebrations among the Jews.

On feast day itself, they dress in elaborate costumes and dance in the streets, a kind of Carnival of Anti-Craziness. Anytime OPC is conquered, it's time for celebration.

The feast itself is a joyful meal shared by family and friends with abundant wine and merriment. Gifts are given to the poor and to each other.

Here is the traditional (though not in the Bible) prayer given after the reading of Esther:

> Blessed are You, Hashem [the Name], our God, King of the Universe, (the God) Who takes up our grievance, judges our claim, avenges our wrong; Who brings just retribution upon all enemies of our soul and exacts vengeance for us from our foes. Blessed are You Hashem, Who exacts vengeance for His people Israel from all their foes, the God Who brings salvation.

It's a great holiday—a holy day when God's people look back and remember his mighty deliverance.

Can you look back on God's mighty deliverance?

Don't say no. It means you're not remembering hard enough.

Remember the prayers he has answered in unexpected ways. Call to mind the craziness of days gone past. Be grateful that you're still here—things might have gone the other way. Thank God for sparing you all the consequences of all your stupid actions. Remember the OPC he has saved you from. The people he has moved out of your life. The problems he has pre-solved before you even showed up.

Do not forget the mercies of the Lord.

Remember. Write them down. Tell a trusted friend. Raise a cup in his honor and bless his name.

Never forget the swamp of OPC that God has brought you through to this point.

Celebrate and say thank you.

Do that over and over and over again, until you actually believe that, with God on your side, OPC has met its match.

One More Thing

In the modern celebration of Purim, a dish is served that holds a secret, special, beautiful, wonderful meaning.

Chicken or meat dumplings.

How's that a wow-factor?

The meat—the good stuff—is hidden inside the noodle, and floating there in a bowl of broth.

The humble dumpling reminds God's people of how God and his grace—the best stuff—is hidden from plain sight. The whole story of Esther shows God mastering the art of hide and seek. He crushes OPC from the shadows. He strengthens the OPC-conqueror from secret places within the soul. He works, unseen and unnoticed. No flash. No spectacles. No overt manifestations.

Like a dumpling, God's finest graces lie hidden beneath a humble surface.

Why?

Maybe it's because if we could see him plainly, we wouldn't need faith.

And God loves faith more than you realize.

God's grace plus your faith yields OPC-kryptonite. Go fight for your life.

𐤔 𐤕 𐤌 𐤗 𐤔 ⊀

Reflections

Reflections 1: Remember to remember God's grace.

Our brains so easily forget the grace we should remember. The Feast of Purim was an annual reminder for God's people to remember—i.e., to call to mind—the grace of God's mighty deliverance.

It wasn't that their memory banks were deleted. It's just that the everyday stuff of life crowded out the mighty acts of God. Yes, that happens. We all know it does.

So did the ancient Jews. So they put something on their calendar to remind them to remember to recall to mind the praise-worthy acts of God. "I would maintain that thanks are the highest form of thought, and that gratitude is happiness doubled by wonder," said G.K. Chesterton. St. Paul advised, "in everything give thanks; for this is the will of God in Christ Jesus for you" (1 Thessalonians 5:18, NKJV).

Gratitude changes you. It adjusts your outlook. It alters your perspective. You can't be thankful and resentful, fearful, or angry at the same time.

Even if you don't *feel* thankful, you can still *say* thank you, and give thanks to God and others.

Write 1 Thessalonians 5:18 on a sticky note, and move it around every week so you don't forget.

Put time for gratitude on your calendar. It could be an hour to write thank you notes, or a tickler to call an old mentor, or a morning to just pray thanksgivings to God.

Next time the negative voices clamor at your soul's committee table, shout them down with thank you's and watch the negatives slither away.

God has been immeasurably gracious to you. How's your memory?

Reflections 2. What fights are you avoiding?

Other People's Craziness banks heavily on you looking the other way. Keeping the peace. Absorbing the insults. Accepting the pain.

The quality of your life depends on the number of difficult conversations you're willing to have.

If you're like me, you have a pacifist gene running its conflict-avoidance stripe right down the middle of your back. For me, it's official. I took a personality quiz. It concluded I live in "Peace Country." I want to make nice with everybody. I don't like conflict, and I don't like fights.

So I became a pastor, go figure.

But if a few decades of pastoring have taught me anything, they have taught me, first of all, that you have to choose your battles. Not all fights are worth fighting. You'll never yank up all the craziness by the roots, and God hasn't called you to try. Ultimately that's his job. Ultimately, that's heaven.

However, some fights are indeed yours to fight. There will come a time when you can no longer avoid them. Avoiding these fights can make things worse. The issues will go underground, turn toxic, and double in power. So...

Have that uncomfortable talk.

Break the silence.

Leave the relationship.

Fight the [metaphorical] fight.

Step into your birthright as a freeborn child of Almighty God.

Winning that fight means nobody else defines you but God. It means you shake off the legacy of victimhood. It means you rise above your own insecurities, weaknesses, and whiny tendencies. It means you make daring choices of faith.

Esther teaches that it's not your environment that determines your level of fulfillment, it's your in-vironment, and the choices you make to seize the life you want.

It's your life.

Go get it.

FOR REFLECTION AND DISCUSSION: What do Philippians 4:6,7 and Colossians 3:17 say about being thankful? What techniques do you use to remind yourself to show gratitude? What fights are you avoiding? What would it look like to engage those battles in peaceful, non-violent ways? What would be the best outcomes? Worst outcomes? What are you going to do about it?

CHAPTER 13

The Last Laugh

ONCE UPON A TIME, A BEAUTIFUL QUEEN was trapped in a crazy castle. Queen Esther survived and thrived. A diabolical Grand Vizier named Haman enacted a fiendish law for an ancient holocaust, calling for the complete annihilation of the Jews. A most nefarious case of OPC.

In a stunning reversal, an Unseen Hand engineers the downfall of the diabolical Haman. Queen Esther and her cousin Mordecai step courageously into the miracle God's grace has already created.

In one of the greatest recorded comebacks in all of history, Haman is impaled on the gallows he built for Mordecai. Mordecai is exalted to the position of second in command, Esther rises up to her full stature as Queen, the Jews are permitted to fight back, and in two days they slaughter enemies that would gladly have slaughtered them.

There is great rejoicing in the land, resulting in a national holiday called the Feast of Purim.

And that brings us to Esther's last chapter, which is only three verses long:

King Xerxes imposed tribute throughout his empire, even to the distant coastlands. His great achievements and the full account of the greatness of Mordecai, whom the king had promoted, are recorded in The Book of the History of the Kings of Media and Persia. Mordecai the Jew became the prime minister, with authority next to that of King Xerxes himself. He was very great among the Jews, who held him in high esteem, because he worked for the good of his people and was a friend at the royal court for all of them. (Esther 10:1-3)

The Shield of Faith

How does the Author end her book about rising above Other People's Craziness?

"King Xerxes imposed tribute throughout his empire."

Taxes!

Even after the smoke clears, Other People's Craziness is still coming at you. You can't get away from it. You can't shield your life from craziness. But you can shield your spirit. Your innermost being. You don't have to put out a welcome mat, and you don't have to let the crazies run your life.

In the New Testament, the Bible describes a savage battle that rages all around us. Bible experts call it spiritual warfare. Good vs. evil. God vs. the Devil. Right vs. wrong. And sane vs. crazy.

We can't blame the devil for all our worries, but he is involved. He's trying to drag you down—even a little. So he's constantly shooting at you. Craziness. Evil. Danger. Wimpiness. OPC.

Sometimes, it seems more than you can handle. But there is a secret weapon, tucked away in Scripture.

[Take] up the shield of faith with which you will be able to extinguish all the flaming arrows of the evil one. (Ephesians 6:16, NAS95)

Flaming arrows. Fiery darts. There they are, sticking out of a wooden shield, like a pin-cushion. Those flaming arrows represent OPC. And that shield represents faith.

The book of Esther was written to buttress your faith. Diving into its depths will put muscle on your faith. That's the point. Esther is a spiritual armory to equip you with the central virtue that can shield your spirit from Other People's Craziness—to equip you with a muscular faith.

Some ancient shields were huge. As big as a door. They protected the whole body. They were made out of planks attached by cross members.

Just like your faith. Faith is not a wimpy little toothpick. It's an interlocking inner confidence made of many parts. Here are six impregnable planks for your OPC-shield.

How to Crazy-Proof Your Spirit

1. Faith in God's explanation of the world and its craziness.

You live in a fallen world, and you're not going to fix that. Don't rage against the system. Don't let it get you down. You've got to accept that the world, even at its best, is not what it's supposed to be. Not what it can be. Not what it one day shall be.

We know that we are of God, and the whole world lies under the sway of the wicked one. (1 John 5:19, NKJV)

> For the creation was subjected to frustration, not by its own choice, but by the will of the one who subjected it, in hope that the creation itself will be liberated from its bondage to decay and brought into the glorious freedom of the children of God. (Romans 8:20, 21, NIV)

What good would it have done Esther to spend her days whining about how unfair life was?

We live in a fallen world.

Some people find this factoid horribly depressing. Bad things happen. Hearts get broken and stomped on. People get used and exploited and abused and cast away. Bad guys seem to get away with it. Good people suffer.

Children get orphaned, and people get sexually exploited, like Esther. People get threatened with genocide, like the Jews. Humans get devalued and pressured to bow to evil, like Mordecai.

It can be discouraging. And that discouragement makes some people rage at God. *It's your fault,* they say. *You could stop this, but you don't.*

And he could, and he doesn't. But there is something greater going on. God is working his cosmic plan, and we just have to trust him.

Because there is coming a day when God will balance the scales of justice. A day in which every evil, every genocidal maniac, every Haman, every Xerxes, every abuser, exploiter, and heartbreaker, will get what's coming.

In the end, OPC goes away. It is healed. Grace wins. Wholeness and health rise above Other People's Craziness.

> And God will wipe away every tear from their eyes; there shall be no more death, nor sorrow, nor crying. There shall be no more pain, for the former things have passed away. (Revelation 21:4, NKJV)

If you want to crazy-proof your spirit, you have to believe that Other People's Craziness isn't ultimate, isn't permanent, isn't dominant, isn't definitive, and isn't triumphant. It is an aberration, and it doesn't belong in your life. When this old world gets folded up, God's going to get rid of it.

2. Faith in God's values no matter what the crazy people may tell you.

When Adolf Hitler came to power, one brave Lutheran pastor named Dietrich Bonhoffer paid with his own money to help Jews escape into Switzerland. He preached fearlessly against the Nazi party.

In 1939 he joined a secret group of high-ranking officers in a conspiracy to assassinate Hitler. The plot was discovered, Bonhoffer was arrested and thrown into a series of concentration camps and prisons.

On April 9, 1945, pastor Dietrich Bonhoffer was executed by hanging.

In what my son terms "high grade irony," in a speech given in 1944, Hitler said, "If the Jews defeat Germany, they will celebrate another Purim." He consciously and insanely saw himself as another Haman strutting across the stage of world history.

So many others bowed to evil, but Bonhoffer would not. Just like Mordecai. When bloodthirsty Haman walked by, Mordecai wouldn't bow.

Why won't Mordecai bow?

3. Because you can't let the crazies run your life.

You'll find this exceptionally difficult when crazy behavior becomes the new normal. As it is on virtually every high school and college campus on earth. Crazy is normal.

Think of how sexual morals have changed in one generation in our country. Virginity used to be a virtue. Now, it's an embarrassment. Premarital sex was frowned upon. Now it's expected and even celebrated. Corruption in government is yawned at. Cheating in college is epidemic.

The new normal is sick.

The new normal breaks hearts.

It is dysfunctional, depressing, and self-destructive.

It celebrates unreality. It is unbiblical.

C.R.A.Z.Y. –Contradicted Reality Always Zaps You.

How did the switch happen so fast?

Simple. Too many people bowed. Sexually. Morally. Financially. Ethically. When humans call normal what God calls sick, the stage is set for heartbreak.

Faith means believing that God's ways are best, even if everybody else thinks you've become weirdly Amish. So what! Don't bow.

I admire the courage any students and young adults who refuse to bow to peer pressure. We live by divine principle (Scripture), not by what our hormonal peers pressure us to do.

We do not seek the path of least resistance. We stick our necks out, take risks, and obey God's Word. We do what is right, and good, and noble, and generous and loving and just— as defined by Scripture—and leave the results to God. It's the only way to lift up that impenetrable shield of faith.

4. Faith that God is there even though he's hiding.

Ten chapters, and not one single mention of God. The words God or Lord or Jesus do not occur in this book even once. Nothing. No God.

It's so totally brilliant, because that's how life usually feels. Heartache comes, and you cry out to God, but all you get back is the echo of your own voice. Where is God? Why God? Help God!

Where were you when the ultrasound tech said our baby's heart stopped beating?

Why did you let that "friend" voice that nasty slander?

Why didn't you stop the economic free-fall that added at least a decade to my working career?

Where were you during the three years it took to diagnose that illness?

Huh, God?

Nothing.

King David struggled with this:

> O God, whom I praise, don't stand silent and aloof while the wicked slander me and tell lies about me. They are all around me with their hateful words, and they fight against me for no reason. I love them, but they try to destroy me— even as I am praying for them! They return evil for good, and hatred for my love. (Psalm 109:1-5)

He was overwhelmed with OPC, and he couldn't find God in the picture. He begged God to not be silent. *God, show yourself. Prove yourself. Fix this.*

How did Esther feel when the soldiers forced her into the King's beauty pageant? When they brought her to his bedroom? When the king selected her? Nobody asked her opinion. Where was God then?

You've got to get your concept of God nailed down till you believe God is present no matter how much he hides. The Bible calls him *Yahweh Shammah,* "The Lord who is There" (Ezekiel 48:35). Even when he's hiding. Even when the pain is intense. Even when your friends think you're crazy. Even when you doubt and question. Even when the numbers don't add up.

God is there.

He will not let you down. He will not forget you or forsake you. He will not let you go. He will not permit you to fall headlong. He will not let evil triumph over you. He will not mess with you. He will not be late to your need. He will not let OPC have the final say.

God will not let the crazies get away with anything in the end. Their day is coming. He may seem to be hiding, but he's intensely active. And he's keeping score. One day all the cosmos will witness the spectacle of his victory and your vindication.

Believe.

5. Faith to take away the welcome mat for OPC.

What will it take to rise above Other People's Craziness?

Sooner or later you have to push back. Esther did, and it triggered a chain reaction of cataclysmic, genocide-averting events. She said no to an exploiter. What an epic moment!

I am fully aware that many times we can't say no to our exploiters. Either we are too young. Too frightened. Too much in danger. Too unsure. I get that. There are times with dealing with OPC calls for tremendous caution and perhaps delay. That caution may very well save your life. If you're in that position, you make sense to me. I encourage that caution.

But realize this: the very caution that enables you to cope in the short term puts out the welcome mat for increasingly dangerous OPC in the long term. So, you've got no choice. You must put together a plan to get out of an abusive and dangerous OPC situation. Call the authorities, get help from a great church, talk to your counselor, work with other family members, find the shelter in town, talk to their leaders, get a new place to live all set up. Then get out.

Pull back the welcome mat. Draw the line.

There is a force in every heart like Xerxes. You would rather avoid the conflict, avoid the nasty results. I understand that. I have it too. But still, sometimes, you have to take the stand and fight. You have to push back against OPC.

But you say, "If I push back, I don't know what he'll do. I can't predict what she'll do! What will my boss, my neighbor, my husband, wife, spouse, ex-, boyfriend, girlfriend, gang, peer group—what will they do! What if..."

And so the excuses flow. Don't let those excuses continue till you're a withered up old person, hunched over, and regretting a life you could have had as it swirls down the toilet of OPC. You are destined for a life of freedom. Believe.

6. Faith that leaves the results to God.

Your job is faith. God's job is outcomes.

God is working a plan. It's bigger than you. It's bigger than any of us. It's a cosmic plan. A plan for the unveiling of a new heavens and new earth, one in which righteousness dwells, and God's people are elevated to heights of joy beyond description.

God is working that plan, and to work that plan he needs certain outcomes in your life and mine. We do not get to determine all of the outcomes. Some, but not all. That's God's business.

Your business is FAITH.

God put you where he put you for such a time as this. He needs you where you are, in this place, and in this time, to work out a cosmic plan for glory and justice and love. It's his plan, and his outcomes. You can ask, but you can't dictate. Leave the results to God.

Here's the trickiest truth of all. It's for mature hearts only. When God's people show faith, sometimes they win the battle, and sometimes they lose. For example:

> Well, how much more do I need to say? It would take too long to recount the stories of the faith of Gideon, Barak, Samson, Jephthah, David, Samuel, and all the prophets. By faith these people overthrew kingdoms, ruled with justice, and received what God had promised them. They shut the mouths of lions, quenched the flames of fire, and escaped death by the edge of the sword. Their weakness was turned to strength. They became strong in battle and put whole armies to flight. Women received their loved ones back again from death... (Hebrews 11:32-35)

Heroes of faith. Winners who came out on top. I'd like to be in this group, please. Their stories get told in Christian media. They have "happily ever after" endings. Yes, that's what I want.

But what about the rest of the paragraph?

> ...But others trusted God and were tortured, preferring to die rather than turn from God and be free. They placed their hope in the resurrection to a better life. Some were mocked, and their backs were cut open with whips. Others were chained in dungeons. Some died by stoning, and some were sawed in half; others were killed with the sword. Some went about in skins of sheep and goats, hungry and oppressed and mistreated. They were too good for this world. They wandered over deserts and mountains, hiding in caves and holes in the ground. (Hebrews 11:35-38)

No thank you.

I don't like these outcomes. OPC triumphed. They failed. Right?

Wrong. Not one molecule of faith in your life is ever a failure. None of it is wasted. Not one puff of faith goes unnoticed by God's all-seeing eye. And it never, ever goes unrewarded. Even the slightest faith reaps an eternal reward of blessings that will one day take your breath away.

> All of these people we have mentioned received God's approval because of their faith, yet none of them received all that God had promised. (Hebrews 11:39)

The world is not worthy of one man or one woman who stands firm in faith for even one shining moment. That is what makes the angels applaud. That moment of faith, that's what makes God smile. And that faith, that courage, that risk, that act, that inaction, that speaking, that keeping silent—whatever the moment calls for—that moment of faith wins the approval of God, and a huge weight of riches and honor and glory in heaven forevermore.

It will be worth it all when we see Jesus.

Victory isn't the victory—faith is the victory.

Heaven is my safe-space.

Until then, I'm stuck inside earth's pain machine. If you base your life with God on getting good outcomes and good results, then OPC will dominate you for that lifetime. The only place where you can be safe from all OPC is heaven, and we're not there yet.

So until that glorious day comes, entrust the results to God. He loves you, and his mercies never fail. In the long run, his results will be immeasurably better than any results you would have created for yourself, even on your best day.

Faith Gets the Last Laugh

Purim is the word for dice, or lots. When Haman chose the day to kill the Jews, he did it by rolling the dice (*purim*).

Haman tossed dice to decide what day to kill all the Jews.

So they call it the Feast of Dice. The very force that is meant to annihilate them becomes something to throw a party over. I'd call that sticking it in the face of their enemies.

Part of overcoming OPC is your ability to laugh at the forces that could destroy you.

You can never be dominated by something you can laugh at. You can never be controlled by someone you can laugh at.

God's people can now laugh at Haman and his stupid dice, and even throw a Feast of Dice, because they had faith that God has the last laugh.

St. Augustine said, "The Cross is the devil's mousetrap."

What did he mean?

Picture Jesus, the precious Son of God. Beloved. Cherished. Picture him coming from heaven to earth. Picture him teaching, loving, serving, living. Fighting to set people free from every form of bondage, including OPC.

Picture him nailed to the Cross. Imagine that moment as hoards of evil spirits roar, cheering the death of the Redeemer. Jesus dies, and is laid in a tomb. And all the powers of hell are concentrated on keeping him there.

His poor, poor disciples. Crushed. Disappointed. Confused. The evil and craziness of their world had destroyed the only inherent Good they knew. They wept. They wrung their hands. They cried on each other's shoulders.

The devil laughed, and the demons rejoiced. And evil did a victory dance. OPC wins again!

But what was God doing?

While evil was celebrating, in that dreary moment, what was God doing?

> He who sits in the heavens shall laugh; The LORD shall hold them in derision. (Psalm 2:4, NKJV)

God was laughing at his enemies.

He was tearing apart the gates of hell, redeeming all those who would accept redemption, erasing their guilt, and breaking death's back.

God was plotting the resurrection to bait Satan and to spring the trap of the devil's personal apocalypse.

God is not wringing his hands when evil seems to triumph. God always gets the final laugh. And if you are in Christ, so do you. OPC doesn't win. Evil doesn't win. God wins, and in him, you are more than a conqueror.

One day, you'll sit in heaven, and review your life from a celestial vantage point.

You will laugh.

You will laugh at your needless drama and overwrought fears.

You will laugh at the idiots who came against you.

You will laugh at how you so often missed the point of God's great love.

You will laugh at ten million prayers that were answered and you failed to notice.

You will laugh at God's spectacular skill of wiping away every tear, and making up for every heartache.

You will laugh when those gargantuan forces of evil that loomed so large on the horizons of your life turn out to be specks of dust on the lens.

You will laugh as you watch God blow them all away.

And you will join that great celestial laugh as God's giant mousetrap finally crushes the head of Evil and hurls that snake, Satan, into a far away place, tumbling head over heels, to shriek his OPC fury forever.

Uncertain Certainties

Esther and Mordecai fight the fight of faith. And for that, they watch as the world makes them great. Greatness comes to them.

But in their greatness, they were still never certain about God. Please don't get me wrong. There are a lot of things I am certain about when it comes to God. They are clearly revealed in his word, and they belong to us (Deuteronomy 29:29).

What I am saying is that on any given day, in any given trial, facing any given OPC, we can never be sure just how God is going to show up.

Even when we are at our Christian best, most of the time, God feels hidden. He feels somewhere in the background. It doesn't seem like he's there at all.

You can be a good Christian. A great Christian, and feel as if God isn't even close to you.

Overcoming OPC does not mean that you have God all figured out.

It simply requires steadily plugging away at a life worth living. Showing up. Being all there. Heart and soul. Laying your life on the line. Feeling your feelings. Wanting your wants. Seizing life. Pressing into your fears. Taking risk.

Exercising shape-shifting, ever-adapting faith.

If Esther teaches us anything, she teaches we have a God who can turn sorrows into joy, mourning into gladness, and death into life. He can turn the stuff that breaks your heart into something you laugh at. He can make you wonder why you were so afraid. He turns Other People's Craziness into Other People's Regrets. He controls kings and their decrees. With one flex of his almighty bicep, he can reverse the irreversible.

The book of Esther begins with a celebration of craziness and ends with a celebration of righteousness, just like the cosmos.

Just like life.

A crazy-proof spirit reposes in God's grip, waiting for that endless Feast of the Last Laugh.

Every day, every hour, and every minute, your God is watching over you. You really can't lose.

Do you want to rise above Other People's Craziness? Make God's Word a bigger voice than the crazies.

Believe the One who shed his blood for you and rose again.

Faith in him never goes unrewarded.

Faith is the victory.

Now go live a bold and daring life worthy of a Great God.

𒈦𒐊𒀭𒐊𒈦𒑐

Reflections

Reflections 1: Learn to separate fulfillment from achievement.

Haman was an achiever. He rose to the top. He checked off every life goal. Yet he was still a miserable S.O.B. (Son of Belial). He had achievement, but not fulfillment.

Ditto for King Xerxes, who conquered much of the known world. He still had to numb his unhappy existence with sexual addiction, alcoholism, indifference to genocide, and a host of other sick "coping mechanisms." He also had achievement, but not fulfillment.

There's a difference.

Achievement is success at checking completed goals off your list.

Fulfillment is the inner satisfaction and contentment you feel from incarnating transcendent values like love, sacrifice, truth, and empathy.

If you're just living for achievement, beware. You might reach the top, but you'll find the ladder leaning against the wrong wall. Look at all the unhappy rich people in our world. Look at the unfulfilled power brokers strutting through halls of power. Consider the broken hearts achieved by sexual liberation. Look at any poor college student, drowning in debt, slogging through a major they picked only for a shot at a lucrative career, even though they hate every minute of every class.

Esther and Mordecai were caught in the vortex of world history. Neither one achieved their goals, at least not the goals they planned for themselves.

But they were both immensely, profoundly, lastingly fulfilled. They found transcendent purpose. They were present, "for such a time as this."

Fulfillment is a treasure money can't buy.

It is the pearl of great price, the by-product of daily choices of love, sacrifice, truth, and empathy.

Yes, go out and achieve your goals.

Just don't forget fulfillment in the process.

"His name is John. Call him John."

I was defending my childhood friend. He'd gotten a nickname that he didn't like. That nickname, which was a screw-up of his last name, sounded like an ethnic slur. But everybody called him that. It was normal.

And that *was* an era of nicknames.

And he didn't seem to mind.

That's just what everybody called him.

Until we became best friends, at around age eleven or twelve, and I asked him about it. "Do you like being called __?"

"Not really," he said.

Even as a kid, I ached for him. From that moment on, every time somebody used the nickname, I corrected them. "Call him John," I said. "That's who he is." I went on a campaign.

It worked. Within a few months, that old nickname faded away. Everyone now called him by his real name—the one given at his birth. The name given by those who loved and nurtured him, a name with meaning, nobility, and virtue.

Her birth name was Hadassah.

Not Esther.

The parents who had hopes for her—the ones who loved and nurtured her till they died, named her Hadassah.

It's the name of a beautiful, glossy, aromatic evergreen shrub that grew in the region. It bloomed with snow-white flowers, dappling the hillsides and perfuming the air. Today that pretty shrub goes by the name, Myrtle.

Maybe her mom and dad took the name from an ancient prophet's promise:

Where once there were thorns, cypress trees will grow. Where briers grew, myrtles [*hadas*] will sprout up. This miracle will bring great honor to the LORD's name; it will be an everlasting sign of his power and love. (Isaiah 55:13)

The myrtle here was something beautiful and desirable, taking the place of something scraggly and wild.

Or perhaps they thought of another hope-filled prophecy:

I will plant trees—cedar, acacia, myrtle [*hadas*], olive, cypress, fir, and pine—on barren land. Everyone will see this miracle and understand that it is the LORD, the Holy One of Israel, who did it. (Isaiah 41:19, 20)

The biblical authors used the myrtle plant to paint a picture of desirability and beauty. It was part of God's beautification project of earth's barren land.

That inspired her parents. When she was born, they named her Hadassah, a name of hope for a more beautiful tomorrow.

But who named her Esther?

We don't know.

And Mordecai had brought up Hadassah, that is, Esther, his uncle's daughter, for she had neither father nor mother... (Esther 2:7, NKJV)

The Hebrew sentence format here is found all over the Old Testament. It is normally used when the older name of a city has to be explained with the newer name. For example: "So Rachel died and was buried on the way to Ephrath (that *is*, Bethlehem). (Genesis 35:19, NKJV, compare Genesis 35:27, Joshua 15:10, Genesis 14:2,3,7). The Author used the linguistic formula that said her older name was Hadassah, but today we call her Esther.

There's no evidence anything nefarious is going on here. It's most probable that Mordecai gave her a new name, a Persian name, because they were stuck in Persia, and he wanted her life to be easier. Esther, in the Persian tongue, means "a star of the night sky."

So what?

Reflections 3: You can be anyone you choose to be, given your unchangeables.

The power is in your hands. OPC doesn't have to name you, define you, own you, confine you, restrict you, marginalize you, victimize you, or homogenize you.

Circumstances made Esther an orphan. Choices made her a queen.

Haman made Mordecai a victim. Choices made him a victor.

Your destiny will not be shaped by wishing, but by choosing.

Not your environment, but your in-vironment, the world you create inside your soul. Your beliefs, values, convictions, non-negotiables.

Other People's Craziness will always suck you into its flow, right down the toilet.

God's Perfect Grace will always empower you to swim upstream, right into the life of your dreams. True happiness. Elusive fulfillment.

It's not your condition, it's your choices, rooted in desire, empowered by grace, enabled by God, pursued with tenacity, rooted and grounded in love.

On that glorious day when you shed the labels of OPC past, your true self will shine. Beautiful, radiant, regal—you will become what you were meant to be. The crazies will still hurl their insults. The trolls will still spit their venom. But you will not be deterred.

Because you are finally stepping into your own skin.

God has given you naming rights to yourself. And you can never find a more life-giving, self-affirming name than "Child of the King."

You are becoming your just right self.

That is what constitutes royalty, no matter your station in life. That is what makes you free, even as you stoop to serve.

You may come from a long line of losers. OPC may hop like fleas from branch to branch of your insane family tree. You may have been molded by addicts, criminals, or dirtbags. Or by filthy rich snobs, arrogant jerks, or self-righteous, condescending prigs.

You may look at your past and want to wish it all away.

A wish is a dark cloud blocking the sun against a bright blue sky.

Wishing has no power. A life of longing will ultimately weaken you.

It's acting that counts. Choosing. Trusting God to be so true that you know everyone else is a liar. Planting one foot in front of the other on the shaky ground of faith, and finding that grace is always there to hold you up.

> Let us therefore come boldly to the throne of grace, that we may obtain mercy and find grace to help in time of need. (Hebrews 4:16, NKJV)

The golden scepter has already been extended. Shed the lies. Shake off the labels. Overcome the fears. Once for all, rise above Other People's Craziness. Come to God. Make him your center of attention. Come to him again and again and again. Daily. Hourly. Come to this endless fountain of supply, of strength, of goodness, and of grace. Come to this shimmering throne.

And you will not only find the welcoming embrace of your nail-scarred Savior. You will also find a treasure you've always hoped for: there, shining with glory, bloodied but unbowed, stronger than you ever thought possible, you will find your truest, richest, deepest Self.

FOR REFLECTION AND DISCUSSION: What are some discoveries you've made about the book of Esther? What are some discoveries you've made about your life? Name a few ways you need to revise your thinking habits about yourself, your God, or your world. How has Esther inspired you to rise to your truest self and highest calling in the world?

𒐖 𒐜 𒈦 𒐚 𒐖 𒐏

I Can Rise Above

It turns out the seeming randomness of Esther's life was part of an intricate plan. Esther was not put in the palace by accident. The twists and turns of your life are not accidents either.

Your Father in heaven has a plan. If you could see it all, it would take your breath away. He is orchestrating events around you in ways you cannot see and cannot imagine.

This is when you have to rest your heart in his loving hands. Faith. You have a God who will never leave you, abandon you, or hurt you.

You may feel weak and uncertain. Unsure. Unloved. Misunderstood. Damaged. Some may seek to hurt and destroy you. You may feel worn out making choices. Confused. Giants of heartbreak and pain may loom large on the horizon.

But you are, with God's power, stronger than all these things. You can defeat these giants. You are royalty. You are amazing and strong and able.

In God's beautiful plan, you are here for such a time as this.

Be bold. Take charge. Live your life to its fullest and trust your God to clean up the mess.

Embrace a confession of grace and faith. Let it be your motto.

I can rise above other people's craziness.

I can rise above abuse.

I can rise above addiction and dysfunction.

I can rise above loneliness.

I can rise above fatigue.

I can rise above too much to do.

I can rise above self-doubt and self-harm.

I can rise above a broken heart.

I can rise above abandonment.

I can rise above illness and sickness and death.

I can rise above injustice.

I can rise above insecurities.

I can rise above my past.

I can rise above the trials yet to come.

I can rise above every fearful giant.

Almighty God is for me. Who can be against me?

I can rise above.

Yes, I can rise.

Acknowledgments

A huge thank you is due to Dr. Glenn Schaefer, professor of Old Testament, emeritus, at Simpson University, for his generous suggestions. You are truly a gentleman and a scholar. Thank you for your quiet strength and wisdom in my life.

I am also grateful to Adaline Coleman and Meridith Chase for their excellent proofreading skills and gracious input. Friends don't let friends proofread their own books. Thank you for helping me look much less silly than I know I can be. Your encouragement means everything to me.

I wish to thank my family at Neighborhood Church, where much of this material was first formed as a sermon series. You've been exceedingly patient with your unworthy pastor, and I am profoundly grateful.

I'm especially grateful for my friend and helper, Gordon DeWitt Jr., who is one hundred percent dedicated to helping me get stuff done. That two percent you mentioned fades to oblivion when I think of all you've done for me.

Margi—you make me better and you made this book better. Thank you for your love, your wisdom, your nudges, your encouragement, your humor, your fun, and your grace. Josie and JD, you light up my heart, and I am proud to be your dad.

Jesus, you loved me first and best, and that is enough for me. May an acknowledgement of your grace never be far from my lips.

Endnotes

[1] Source: http://www.snopes.com/business/consumer/nordstrom.asp, retrieved April 7, 2013.

[2] Bob Gillam. "The Importance of Fellowship in a New Testament Church." http://www.bible.org/page.php?page_id=437.

[3] Adam Clarke. *Commentary on the Bible.* 1813. Public Domain. *loc. cit.*

[4] Shoda, Y., Mischel, W., Peake, P. K. (1990). Predicting adolescent cognitive and self-regulatory competencies from preschool delay of gratification: Identifying diagnostic conditions. Developmental Psychology, 26(6), 978–986.

[5] A. W. Tozer, "Knowledge of the Holy", pg. 93

[6] B.B. Warfield, *Election.* A pamphlet published by Presbyterian Board of Publication in 1918. Online at: http://www.the-highway.com/Election_Warfield.html

[7] John Piper, *The Pleasures of God.* P. 252.

[9] *The Christ Life for the Self Life,* pp. 94-96.

[10] Arthur F. Holmes, "The Just War." Intervarsity Christian Fellowship, retrieved December 30, 2016. http://intervarsity.org/news/the-just-war

[11] Ibid.